Wine Lovers Cookbook

Audrey Ellis

WINE LOVERS COOKBOOK

Hutchinson of London

By the same author
(Published by Stanley Paul)

Farmhouse Kitchen
Kitchen Garden Cook Book

Hutchinson & Co (Publishers) Ltd
3 Fitzroy Square, London W1

London Melbourne Sydney Auckland
Wellington Johannesburg Cape Town
and agencies throughout the world

First published 1975
© Audrey Ellis 1975
Drawings © Hutchinson & Co
(Publishers) Ltd 1975

Filmset by BAS Printers Limited
Wallop, Hampshire
and printed by The Broadwater Press
Welwyn Garden, Herts

ISBN 0 09 120760 6

Illustrations by Kate Simunek
Diagrams by Illustra Design

Photography

John Lee at John Lee Studio
Roy Rich at Angel Studio

Credits

Princes Foods Limited
(opposite page 32)
Baxters of Speyside
(opposite page 33)
Spanish Olives
(page 47 and opposite page 48)
New Zealand Lamb Information Bureau
(opposite page 49 and page 73)
Gale's Honey
(page 61)
Hassy Perfection Celery
(page 69)
Irish Dairy Board
(page 77)
German Food Centre
(page 78)
British Sausage Bureau
(page 81)
Colman's Mustard
(page 85)
Buxted
(page 89 and opposite page 96)
Dutch Dairy Bureau
(page 93)
Birds Eye Foods Limited
(opposite page 97)
Mateus Rosé
(opposite page 112)
Cinzano
(opposite page 113)
Aveleda
(page 115)

Contents

Introduction

Wine is one of the good things of life, and better still when enjoyed in company.

Drinking wine together makes conversation flow more easily, and many a shy friendship has flowered over a convivial glass of wine. Even opening the bottle is a nice little ceremony, and the sound of the cork being drawn promises pleasure.

A meal served with wine, however simple the menu, is a social occasion. It improves good humour, polishes wit, and makes the food of an averagely gifted cook taste delicious. Do not confuse this sober fact with alcoholic euphoria. Wine and food are such perfect partners that one enhances the other, and many dishes are infinitely improved by the addition of wine.

It used to take nerve to pour a reckless half pint of wine into a casserole, when it came from the only bottle in the house, and was worth its weight in gold. Today one can pour with a clear conscience and a steady hand – half a pint seems such a small loss from a whole litre. It is the one precious ingredient I use regularly in cooking (apart from cream and the marvellous mushroom) which has remained relatively cheap and stable in price. Personally, I use wine lavishly and often, have not yet felt the pinch of want, and everything I put it in is the better for it.

Wine either for drinking or cooking is no longer considered a decadent extravagance, by any standards. Compared with other enjoyable things, it is not even dear. Some noble wines, through the pressure of world demand, have risen alarmingly in cost. Others, less familiar, will have to take their places on our tables. But the habit of drinking wine, probably at first encouraged by holidays abroad, is firmly established, and many households now boast a small stock, or, as the French call it, *libraire de vins*.

A modest start can be made by buying the non-vintage branded wines which are skilful blends aimed at balancing out and correcting the variations of different vintages. This means that, having discovered a wine and a brand you enjoy, you can always be certain that its character will please you, and for sheer value I know no better way to spend your money. But the true wine lover will not be happy without making more adventurous voyages in the world of wine. And if necessary making mistakes, before he finds certain individual wines with a personality which 'speak' to him (or her) in a special way. For yourself, your nearest and dearest, or a small gathering you wish to impress, it is wise to remember that the few extra pence which bring the bottle up to or over a pound may be extraordinarily well spent; about five-sixths of the total cost consists of duty, the cost of bottling, and then conveying the bottle to you. Another fifteen pence on the shop price may be doubling the amount you pay for the *wine itself*.

Time was when the choice and serving of wine was distinctly a male province. The master of the house brought home a couple of bottles, a mysterious bulge in his briefcase, to grace the occasional dinner party; jealously guarding for himself the privilege of opening and pouring the wine. The ladies got one glass apiece, and the men somehow finished the rest. Very few women in this country bought wine at all, and would have considered it a ruinous luxury to cook with it. Besides, they did not know how, and were timid about learning. A friend who made the classic *Coq au vin rouge* for the first time with a whole bottle of Burgundy, frankly expected the entire company to slide under the table in a drunken stupor.

But times have changed, and for the better. Women, who now buy nearly half the wine sold, crowd the wine appreciation classes, take a keen interest in understanding wine, and form their own tastes and preferences.

No wonder bored wine waiters always used to suggest something white and on the sweet side for the ladies, no matter what they were eating. Experience is the best developer of an appreciative palate, and most women begin by enjoying a fairly sweet wine, then, if given the chance, graduate to the enjoyment of drier white wines and full-bodied reds. It is all a question of education. It takes time for a child's taste to progress from sweetened milk with a dash of coffee to the real thing, and women need a fair chance to develop adult tastes in wine. A sweet white wine has its proper place, of course; but it is not the ideal choice with every dish, on the grounds that the little woman knows no better.

There is no great mystery about using wine in the kitchen. In countries where it is an integral part of daily life, it has always been the custom to cook adventurously with wine, and to try out whether adding a generous glassful at the beginning of cooking, or stirring in some separately reduced wine as an afterthought, might improve a dish.

Cooking with wine is a joy because it is so easy. Whatever the method, by slow or fast evaporation, the aim is to drive off the alcohol, and leave only the residual flavour of the wine – rich and robust, or light and delicate – just, so to speak, the soul of the grape.

For wine itself is said to have a soul, in France at least, where the appreciation of wine is something between a religion and a lifelong love affair. In fact a good red Burgundy is spoken of admiringly as 'having love', *un vin qui a de l'amour*. A Sauternes might be described as having a taste like the slow unfolding in the mouth of a peacock's magnificent tail, *comme une queue de paon*, but that is by the way. The languages of love and of wine have always been curiously entwined, perhaps because wine is the happy symbol of all that is enjoyable in life. The song writer of today echoes poets through the ages when he claims a woman's lips are 'much sweeter than wine'; still the ultimate compliment!

This book does not pretend to make you an expert on wine, but it might well serve as an introduction to its study. If you feel tempted, I have included information on good books to read, clubs you could join, and courses available such as evening classes in wine appreciation.

As well as providing a repertoire of more than two hundred recipes covering the whole exciting range of wine cookery, this book has something to offer those who, without exacting study, would like to acquire more wine expertise generally; to know, for example, what certain terms on a label mean, and, when you have bought the wine of your choice, how to store and serve it correctly, and even which glasses to use.

Since wine lovers are gregarious people who like entertaining, much of the advice and most of the recipes are concerned with receiving one's friends and giving them sustenance. I have already spoken of wines to serve the cherished few, but I hope you will find useful my suggestions on working out the quantities needed to feed and give festive drink to a considerable number of people. Fortunately, the availability of litre and even larger bottles makes this far less costly than in years gone by, when a punch or cup had to be frantically watered down with lemonade if late-comers turned up. Mixed drinks based on wine, which often form the focal point of a party, can be quite cheap. But that is not the note on which to end the introduction to this book. We do not love wine, want to drink it more often, and cook with it too, because it is a sophisticated foible of the rich (as it well may be, for you can pay more than a hundred pounds for a dozen bottles) or because it represents cheap merriment.

If we are becoming a wine-drinking nation, it is not because we are poor, or wealthy, but discerning. We have discovered wine to be one of the great joys of living, and worth every penny we pay for it.

AUDREY ELLIS

Some useful facts and figures

Spoon measure conversions to ounces

	Imperial tablespoons	oz	American measures
butter	$1\frac{1}{2}$	1	2 tablespoons
breadcrumbs (dried)	6	1	$\frac{1}{4}$ cup
breadcrumbs (fresh)	7	1	$\frac{1}{2}$ cup
cornflour	2	1	$\frac{1}{4}$ cup cornstarch
plain or self-raising flour	3	1	$\frac{1}{4}$ cup sifted all-purpose self-raising or cake flour
rice	2	1	cup
sugar (caster)	2	1	cup granulated
sugar (demerara)	2	1	cup brown, firmly packed
sugar (icing)	4	1	$\frac{1}{4}$ cup sifted confectioners'

3 teaspoons equal 1 tablespoon

Liquid: If no measuring jug is available, 8 British tablespoons equal $\frac{1}{4}$ Imperial (20 fl oz) pint.

Liquid metric measures:
1 litre – $1\frac{3}{4}$ pints (2 American pints + 3 fl oz)
$\frac{1}{2}$ litre – 1 demilitre ($17\frac{1}{2}$ fl oz) (1 American pint + 3 tablespoons)
$\frac{1}{10}$ litre – 1 decilitre ($3\frac{1}{2}$ fl oz) (scant $\frac{1}{2}$ cup)
$\frac{1}{100}$ litre – 1 centilitre ($\frac{1}{3}$ fl oz) (2 American teaspoons)

Bottle sizes and measures

British	American
Measure (spirits) – $\frac{4}{5}$ fl oz	$\frac{4}{5}$ fl oz
Measure (liqueurs) – $\frac{4}{5}$ fl oz	$\frac{4}{5}$ fl oz
Miniatures – 2-3 tablespoons	3–4 tablespoons
	Split – 6.4 fl oz
Standard half bottle – 13 fl oz	Tenth – 12.8 fl oz
Standard bottle – $1\frac{1}{3}$ pints	Fifth – 25.6 fl oz
Litre bottle – $1\frac{3}{4}$ pints	Pint bottle – 16 fl oz
2-litre bottle – $3\frac{1}{2}$ pints	Quart bottle – 32 fl oz
Flagon – $\frac{1}{2}$ gallon (80 fl oz)	$\frac{1}{2}$ gallon jug – 64 fl oz
Champagne bottle – 80 centilitres (1 pint 8 fl oz)	1 gallon jug – 128 fl oz
Magnum – 2 standard bottles	Magnum – 52 fl oz
Jereboam – 4 standard bottles	Jereboam – 104 fl oz
Methuselah – 8 standard bottles	Methuselah – 208 fl oz

Metric conversion chart for dry foods

oz	Approx. grammes to nearest whole figure	Recommended conversion to nearest unit of 25 grammes	oz	Approx. grammes to nearest whole figure	Recommended conversion to nearest unit of 25 grammes
1	28	25	6	170	175
2	57	50	8	226	225
3	85	75	10	283	275
4	113	125	12	340	350
5	142	150	16	456	450

To convert quantities over 16 oz to grammes, add together the number of oz from the chart and the equivalent number of grammes, thus 20 oz = 569 grammes, converted to the nearest unit of 25, 575 grammes. (1 kilogramme = 100 grammes.)

Comparative scales for wine and spirit strengths

The strength of wine or spirit depends on its alcohol content, measured by three different scales. In France the Gay Lussac scale is used. This is divided into 100 parts, thus giving the *percentage* of alcohol in wine. Therefore a wine with 10 parts of alcohol to 90 parts water has a 10% alcohol content.

In Great Britain, the Sykes scale was formerly used. This is divided into 175 parts, giving the alcohol content in *degrees proof*. Therefore a wine containing 10° alcohol is 17.5° proof. (Since our entry into the EEC, we have adopted the Gay Lussac scale.) In America, another scale is used. This is divided into 200 parts, so that a wine containing 10% alcohol is 20° proof.

Comparative table

	Water	Table Wines	Fortified Wines	Normal Spirits	Pure Alcohol
Gay Lussac	0%	10%–15%	$18\frac{1}{2}$%–25%	40%–50%	100%
Sykes (proof)	0°	17.5°–25°	30°–47.5°	70°–87.5°	175°
American (proof)	0°	20°–30°	35°–50°	80°–100°	200°

The 'proof' scale derives from older times when customs officers would test the strength of a spirit by pouring it over gunpowder and igniting it. If the gunpowder burned it was proof that the liquid contained sufficient alcohol.

Rating	°F.	°C.	Gas Mark
Very cool	225	110	$\frac{1}{4}$
	250	130	$\frac{1}{2}$
Cool	275	140	1
	300	150	2
Moderate	325	170	3
	350	180	4
Moderately hot	375	190	5
	400	200	6
Hot	425	220	7
	450	230	8
Very hot	475	240	9

Table on left gives equivalent Fahrenheit, Celsius (new electric cookers) and Gas Mark temperatures.

Take a leaf from this book

This symbol throughout indicates a useful hint on wine cookery or my personal choice of a wine to accompany a particular dish.

Courses and books on wine appreciation

The International Wine and Food Society has a Young Members Group, for those under the age of 35; members under the age of 25 pay a reduced annual subscription of £2.10 and are excused the entrance fee. The standard annual subscription is £4.20, and an entrance fee of £2.10, which covers husband-and-wife joint membership, for whom the annual subscription together is £5.25 (prices exclusive of VAT). The Society sends you without charge a magazine and offers dinners, luncheons, wine tastings, a wine bulletin, cooking demonstrations, international gastronomic conventions and weekends, wine and food tours and many other interesting events.

Courses in wine appreciation are available to members and consist of five evening sessions, spread out over three weeks. The first four sessions are held at the Junior Carlton Club, Pall Mall, London, S.W.1. and each includes two lectures, wine tastings and refreshments. The final session includes two lectures and concludes with a dinner illustrating the marriage of wine and food and is held at the Society's offices. The cost approaches £41.50 but wives accompanying husbands only pay half price. Lecturers include Masters of Wine.

For further information apply to The Secretary, International Wine and Food Society, Marble Arch House, 44 Edgware Road, London, W.2. Tel: 01-402 6212.

One-day Introductory and three-day Intermediate courses on wines and spirits are organized under the auspices of Gilbey Vintners at their school of wine, where you have the opportunity to extend your knowledge under modern conditions and receive tuition from an experienced team of lecturers including a Master of Wine. The courses are full-day sessions and include wine tastings, coffee, lunch and tea. For further information apply to The Principal, Mr. Clive Williams, Gilbey Vintners School of Wine, 32 Aybrook Street, London, W.1. Tel: 01-935 4446.

In the London area alone seven colleges of adult education offer evening courses in wine appreciation.

Central London Institute, 6 Bolt Court, Fleet Street, London, E.C.4.

Central Wandsworth Institute, Mansfield School, West Hill, London, S.W.15.

Chelsea/Westminster Institute, Marlborough School, Sloane Avenue, London, S.W.3.

Dulwich Institute, William Penn School, Red Post Hill, London, S.E.24.

Fulham and S. Kensington Institute, Beaufort House School, Lillie Road, London, S.W.6.

Greenwich Institute, Kidbrooke School, Corelli Road, London, S.E.3.

Stanhope Institute, Fitzroy Place, Longford Street, London, N.W.1.

For information on local courses and wine societies, consult your public library.

Bibliography

For serious study of wine the following books offer extremely good value for their respective price brackets.

A WINE PRIMER, André Simon (Penguin) 30p.

WINES, Fichel (Penguin) 40p.

THE ENJOYMENT OF WINE, H. W. Yoxall (Michael Joseph) £2.50.

THE SUBTLE ALCHEMIST: a book of wine, George Rainbird and Ronald Searle (Michael Joseph) £2.75.

THE WORLD ATLAS OF WINE, Hugh Johnson (Mitchell Beazley) £9.50.

Wines of the World

The temperate zones favourable to growing grapes for making wine exist around the world both north and south of the equator. Because of the high proportion of land masses in the northern hemisphere, more wine is made there than in the southern hemisphere, where the temperate zone includes more ocean, and parts of Australia, South Africa and South America almost exclusively. Many excellent wines are unknown outside their country of origin, and some European wines are unfamiliar even in Britain because they are exported in very small quantities or not at all. Few people here have had the opportunity to taste Crimean or Bulgarian wines.

For reasons of trade preferences, wines from Australia and South Africa are available here in moderate quantities. But you would be lucky to have the chance of tasting the excellent Chilean wines.

The wines of America

American readers may justly be proud of their own domestic and varietal wines.

Wine is grown in commercial quantities in twenty out of the fifty American states but over 80% of the wine produced in America comes from the state of California. The climate differs less from year to year in California than it does in European wine growing countries, making the vintage less important.

Nevertheless much of the wine is made from the same varieties of grape and by the same time-honoured methods, and the finest wines compare very favourably with their European equivalents. I have visited a Californian winery in the famous Napa Valley and seen wine being fermented first in vats of the native redwood, then in oak vats from Germany which were more than a hundred years old.

American wines contain a maximum 14% alcohol (including sparkling wines) and there are three major classifications – generic, cooking and varietal wines.

Generic wines Named after districts in Europe producing wine of similar characteristics, or according to their colour. Several grape varieties are blended and the taste may vary considerably according to the vintner. These are the wines usually used both for cooking and drinking. Typical examples are: Among the whites – Chablis, Rhine Wine, White Chianti. Californian Sauternes are not all sweet, some (labelled dry) are very dry indeed. Among the reds – Burgundy, Vino Rosso Mountain Red, Barbarone. The cost is similar to our blended *vins ordinaires*.

Cooking wines Cheaper than generic wines because salt has been added to make them unpalatable to drink. This practice, which originated in restaurant kitchens to discourage tippling by chefs and waiters, is now carried out to a government specification and the wine attracts less tax.

Note: Recipes in this book will require to be adjusted to allow for the additional salt in American cooking wines.

Varietal wines Named for the type of grape from which they are made and must contain a minimum of 51% of that grape variety. Most contain far more. The wines must also embody the aroma, flavour and colour distinctive of the particular grape.

Typical examples are: Among the whites – Johannesburg Riesling, Sylvaner, Chenin Blanc, Pinot Chardonnay. Of the reds – Gamay, Zinfandel, Ruby Cabernet, which are light bodied and intended to be drunk fairly young. Cabernet Sauvignon is a bordeaux type, and Pinot Noir a burgundy; both improve with age. There are also varietal pinks from California, mainly Gamay Rosé and Grenache Rosé.

Bottle sizes: These wines are available in the standard size bottles and also in half gallon or gallon jugs and other large sizes, of which the most popular is the magnum.

Sparkling wines Californian champagne labelled 'natural' is completely dry, brut – dry, extra dry – has a hint of sweetness. Dry, sec and demi-sec – medium, noticeably or very sweet, respectively. The same methods, including the time consuming *méthode champenoise*, are used to produce sparkling wines in America as in Europe. Wines that have been mechanically aerated are labelled carbonated wine.

Typical examples are: Champagne, Sparkling Burgundy, Crackling Rosé and Sparkling Muscat.

Interpreting wine labels

Wine labels are a fascinating study. Consider the delightful label with a charming view of a picturesque Château bearing the following words. Above the picture, 'Domaines du Château de Beaune'; on the left, 'Produce of France' (see page 61). Beneath this on the left is a little saying 'Il n'est bon Pain que de Froment, il n'est vin que de Beaune!' Wine lore is full of such delightful examples.

On the whole, the more closely defined the description of the place where the wine was made, the more expensive and (if produced in a good, named year) the better you can expect it to be.

Here is an example, taking claret, and the description on the label according to the quality of the wine.

It might bear the words 'Château Margaux' or, going down the quality scale, 'Haut Médoc' (since wines of the Haut Médoc are considered finer than those of the Bas Médoc), or 'Médoc', or at the bottom of the quality scale, simply 'Bordeaux'. Less specific still is 'Vin Ordinaire Rouge de France'. Only wines from the Bordeaux region are called claret by the British, derived from the French word *clairet*, meaning clear, light and bright.

In the same way, burgundies labelled 'Côte de Beaune' or 'Côte de Nuits', are better quality than those labelled 'Côte de Beaune Villages' or 'Côte de Nuits Villages'.

Wineupmanship

Wine is worth a little study, even if you have no ambition to become a wine expert and quite to the contrary, a firm determination not to become a wine snob. Knowing enough about wine to appraise and appreciate it, and discuss it knowledgeably, is one of today's social accomplishments. It is unnecessary to go, as the schoolboy put it, *le cochon complet*. You may never be able to distinguish a Château Latour from a Château Lafite; you may never come to the conclusion that any wine must be drunk 'reverently, bareheaded and on one's knees', or think that another will improve 'when it has pulled in its ends a little'. You will continue to drink what pleases you at a price you can afford whatever the wine pundits say. But for a wine lover, there is a considerable pleasure in developing one's expertise on the subject.

Table wines These are the red, white and rosé wines made by natural processes of fermentation from black or white grapes, or a combination of both, which you drink with food; the alcohol content varies between 9% and 15% (French Gay Lussac scale). Some wines are so precious it would be absurd to say that they are suitable for cooking. (You could always use vintage wines past their prime, or the lees in a bottle, strained through muslin.) On the other hand, do not use very cheap, vinegary or sour wine hoping that cooking will disguise the flavour or lack of it. It will not. Dry still cider can be substituted for dry white table wine, and in sweet dishes where the addition of a sweet or sparkling white wine is indicated, sweet cider. But it does give food that faint taste of the apple, not by any means a bad thing.

Sparkling and semi-sparkling wines These are wines where man takes a more positive part in the wine making process. By retaining part of the carbon dioxide naturally produced by fermentation, the wine (whether red, white or rosé) becomes sparkling or semi-sparkling.

The famous *méthode champenoise* is costly because this long and complicated process is controlled in the bottle itself.

Fortified wines As the name suggests, these wines have a higher alcoholic content than table wines because grape brandy is added to them. Thus fortified they have a more concentrated flavour (and a longer life when opened and exposed to the air) because of the higher alcoholic content, which varies between 18% and 25%. Such wines are usually drunk before or after a meal rather than with food, but are invaluable as an ingredient in cooking. Very sweet fortified wines would not be offered immediately before eating as they cloy the palate. Sherry, Madeira, Marsala, Malaga and port are the great fortified wines. Other lesser known ones are Californian angelica, similar to white port, Californian Tokay, *vins doux naturels* from France, and *pineau*.

Apéritif wines These are blended wines to which some spirit and a variety of herbs, berries and other natural flavourings are added. They are lighter than fortified wines (not more than a 16% alcoholic content) and are intended to stimulate the appetite. (Dry vermouth for savoury cooking, sweet vermouth for desserts; Pernod with its strong anise flavour, is used very sparingly, mostly with fish.) Vermouths, both French and Italian, sweet and dry, are prime favourites and there are many branded varieties. Quinine is added to Dubonnet and Byrrh and Lillet has Armagnac.

Liqueurs Usually made from grape spirit to which sugar syrup colouring and flavourings are added, and are offered with coffee in small glasses to round off a good meal. One exception, the stately Drambuie, is based on whisky, heather honey and herbs. The fruit flavoured brandies, apricot, cherry, peach and so on are termed 'ladies' favourites'. So are Tia Maria, Crème de Cacao – coffee and chocolate liqueurs. Crème de Menthe has an innocent peppermint flavour. Cointreau, Curaçao and Grand Marnier, all orange flavoured, are useful in cooking as well as for drinking; so are Kirsch and Maraschino with their flavour of bitter cherries. To save you from confusing flavourings with liqueurs, remember that Bitters, Angostura, the French Amer Picon, and Italian Fernet Branca, have a base of herbs and were originally intended to be used medicinally. Nowadays they are used to flavour cocktails and gin based drinks, such as Pink Gin, made from ice, Angostura bitters, gin and water.

Spirits Not all are distilled from wine, but all are liquids of high alcoholic strength made by distilling liquids of low alcoholic strength. For example rum, distilled from fermented molasses and the by-products of sugar refining, is both drunk as a spirit and used in sweet cooking. Gin is distilled from grain and flavoured with juniper berries. Whisky is always made from grain cereals, which vary according to the country and area of origin. Vodka can be made from either grain, usually rye, malt, or potato starch.

Brandy is distilled from grape wine, and is considered the king of spirits. The true French Cognac is made from grapes grown only in a strictly delineated area. First class brandy is known as *fin* or *fine champagne*; *eau-de-vie* and *marc* are rougher but have a great deal of flavour. Armagnac, made in Gers, is another sort of brandy. Fruit brandies, such as slivovitz and kirsch, are distilled from fruit wine and Calvados from cider. After cider making the pulp is used to make a local *marc*.

The French wine classes

Although the glossary may help you to steer your way among 'Châteaux' and 'Domaines', 'Clos' and 'Cuve Close', some important terms remain to be explained.

French table wines have long been subject to strict laws as to the description on the label, and the initials A.O.C. or V.D.Q.S. are already familiar to most wine lovers. Here is a fuller explanation.

Appellation d'origine controlée (A.O.C.)

This mark offers a double guarantee of origin and quality (within the limits of the vintage) and indicates that the wine comes not only from the specified place but that it is made according to the local practice.

Vins délimités de qualité superieure (V.D.Q.S.)

This mark indicates a wine of superior quality from one of the lesser known regions, and the wine must fulfil stringent conditions regarding the area of production, the vines, methods of growing and wine making, the maximum yield and the alcohol content.

The new German wine classes

The three divisions of quality have been decided to conform with the EEC community's law, with special consideration of the frequent necessity to add sugar to the grape juice before fermentation because of the uncertain climate (and lack of sunshine in some years) where most German wines are produced. The sweetening may be sugar or 'süss reserve'; wine with a very high sugar content is pasteurised and stored for the purpose.

1. Deutscher Tafelwein

These wines may be sweetened and blended from four specific German wine regions. If a bottle contains 75% of the wine of one region it may bear that region's name.

2. Qualitätswein bestimmter Anbaugebiete (Q.b.A.)

A full-bodied wine typical of the region and originating solely from one of the eleven specific regions. The label has to show the official certification number. Preconditions: character typical for the region and grape variety, without blemish in terms of appearance, bouquet, and flavour. Liebfraumilch is now considered a generic name and all wines labelled 'Liebfraumilch' must therefore fall into this category.

3 Qualitätswein mit Prädikat

The rarest and most elegant of wines. Origin solely from one of the restricted subregions. Further restrictions such as: registered harvest date, higher natural concentration of must (therefore complete lack of added sugar), strict control by means of an analysis and degustation (colour, clarity, bouquet, taste).

4. *Naturwein*

These are wines which have not been sweetened but are not qualified for any of the three classifications.

(Wines merely labelled 'Tafelwein' may contain up to 15% of wine from other EEC countries.) The following additional label titles will only be applied to Prädikat wines:

(i) *Spätlese* – made from late picked grapes.
(ii) *Auslese* – made from selected bunches of such grapes.
(iii) *Beerenauslese* – made from selected bunches which have been affected by 'noble rot'.
(iv) *Trockenbeerenauslese* – as in (iii) but the grapes have shrivelled to a raisin-like state.
(v) *Eiswein* – rare wines made from grapes harvested and crushed while still frozen.

Hock is any wine from areas adjoining the Rhine, for example the Rheingau and the Palatinate. Typical German titles are as follows:

'Erbacher' – from Erbach in Rheingau.
'Marcobrunn' – from the Marcobrunn vineyard in Erbach.
'Riesling' – named simply for the grape variety.
'Kabinett' – wines of superior quality.

The new Italian wine classes

Italy, the largest producer of wine in the world, enjoys a more settled climate and higher proportion of sunny weather than Germany or France. Her definitions are the *Denominazione d'Origine*.

1. *Semplice*

These wines are locally made by the traditional local method (D.O.S.).

2. *Controllata*

These wines are controlled by a specific production figure, specified types of grapes and method of vinification (D.O.C.).

3. *Controllata e Garantita*

Special wines sold in bottles or containers with a capacity of not more than 5 litres which bear a governmental seal. These wines must conform to the *Controllata* regulations.

Sherry

Sherries are matured by the Cradera and Solera system, in which wine is brought forward, from the younger to the older casks, never transferring more than one third of the contents, over a number of years, to the stage when it will be mature. Sherries enter the blending system after fermenting out to a dry pale white wine, at the *Anada* (wine of the year) stage. Some of these sherries develop *flor*, which produces Fino characteristics, and those which do not develop flor become Oloroso sherries. Sweet and dark sherries are produced by the addition of colouring and extremely sweet wines, also matured in Soleras. Here are their names and descriptions.

Fino – pale dry sherry.

Manzanilla – Fino sherry matured near the coast at Sanlucar; it has a salty slightly bitter tang.

Montilla – Dry sherry from Cordoba, with a little more alcohol than a Fino.

Amontillado – Has gained colour and depth of flavour from age, and is not so dry as a Fino.

Commercial Amontillado – Medium dry sherry made by mixing Oloroso and Fino sherries with colour and sweet wines.

Oloroso – Dry, dark sherry, drunk as a desert wine.

Golden Oloroso – Sweet.

Cream – Dark golden sweet Oloroso sherry.

Brown – Very dark, very sweet Oloroso sherry. Only sherries of high quality are further matured in the bottle and bear the date of bottling.

Port

Wood ports are matured only in cask, and classed as follows.

White port – Matured about two years, golden in colour, and may vary from dry to sweet.

Ruby port – A blend of young and old ports, average age of three to five years, dark ruby in colour, with a rich sweet taste.

Tawny port – An older and therefore browner port, at least 12 years matured, lighter and more delicate in flavour. Cheaper ones are made by blending ruby and white ports together. Old tawnies become pale as colour is lost by long maturing in cask. Vintage ports are matured in cask for 2 years, then at least 10 years in bottle.

Vintage port – Best port of a fine year, between 12 and 20 years old. Ruby colour is due to colour loss by long maturation in

bottle. The deposit thrown is called the 'crust' and it must be decanted, stoppered and drunk as unlike other ports it loses its bouquet and taste very quickly.

L.B.V. – Indicates a late bottle vintage not quite of above standard. Matured in cask from 4 to 6 years, but not necessarily further matured in bottle.

Crusted port – A blend of good ports from different years, aged both in cask and bottle, which needs decanting.

Port is served at the end of a formal dinner and is passed round the table, always to the left, so that each diner helps himself and passes on the decanter to his neighbour presumably until it is empty or all the diners have slipped beneath the table. Ladies used to be expected to leave the room, presumably so that they should not witness this disgraceful scene, or hear the bawdy stories that traditionally accompany the ritual.

(Port and lemon is a mixed drink unjustly considered vulgar. I confess to having drunk it myself to the horror of my escort who described it as 'Charwoman's Ruin'.)

Madeira

Madeira is usually made on the Solera system, like sherry, but lasts for a great deal longer – Madeira made in 1789 is still excellent. There are four different types of Madeira, named after the grapes from which they are produced.

Sercial – Pale dry with an aromatic flavour.

Verdelho – Golden dry, medium rich.

Bual or *Boal* – Brown and rich.

Malmsey or *Malvazia* – Fine old tawny darker than any other.

All styles of wine are matured in *Estufas* (large vats kept in hot rooms for several months at as high as 140°F). This 'backing' of the wine imparts the traditional burnt flavour of Madeira and gives it a rich colour.

Solera Madeira – This is matured in a solera system like sherry. But any date on the bottle is only the year the Solera was started, not the vintage.

Cognac is labelled very specifically to guarantee age but not quality. The age is indicated by stars (one star not less than three years, two stars not less than four years, three stars not less than five, usually at least seven) and by letters with the following meaning:

V.S.O. – very special old: between 12 and 17 years.
V.S.O.P. – very special old pale: between 18 and 25 years.
V.V.S.O.P. – very, very special old pale: between 25 and 40 years.
X.O., Cordon Bleu, etc., are house equivalents of V.V.S.O.P.

The art of wine tasting

To judge the character of a wine, the senses of sight, smell and taste are all employed.

Sight: Hold the wine glass up to the light. A cut glass shows up the colour and brilliance but any well-polished plain glass of the appropriate shape will do; coloured glass will falsify the colour and prevents any appraisal of the appearance of the wine. White wines run the entire gamut of shades of yellow, from the pale and delicate greenish tints, through straw colour, light and dark golden, to an exquisite amber. One expects a vinho verde to be faintly greenish (the technical term is citron) and a Sauternes would be disappointing if too pale a yellow. Red wines may be light or dark with shades ranging from purple (when young) to the jewel tones of ruby and garnet. Burgundies are the deepest and richest red of all. Rosé wines may be pale pink, a slightly deeper pink or even have a coppery tone like the sparkling rosés of Portugal. Some resemble the fruit of the apricot more than they do the rose. The colour is known in France as the *robe*, or dress.

Descriptive terms: favourable – clear, brilliant, gleaming; unfavourable – cloudy, pale, faded, dull. All wines darken with age; the whites towards amber, the reds towards tawny brown.

Smell: Time must be allowed to test the bouquet or 'nose' of the wine which may be strong, delicate, or refreshing. Have the glass only half filled, rotate the glass slowly to roll the wine round the sides and release its scent. Full-bodied wines smell rich but certain wines have an aroma that is reminiscent of fruit or flowers. A red Chinon reminds one of violets and a white Gewurtztraminer recalls a bunch of fragrant meadow flowers and herbs. Poor wines smell of little but vinegar.

Descriptive terms: favourable – fine, perfumed, fruity, spicy, seductive; unfavourable – flat, corky, burned, peppery, dumb, acetic, tart, peardrops. This last term, of a young white wine, means it is badly made and probably undrinkable.

Taste: The flavour of the wine gives an experienced taster the most information about its exact origin. Great experience may enable you to tell not only exactly where it was produced but its age, the type of grape from which it was made and the method employed. Fortunate is the wine lover who has an opportunity to develop his or her palate to such a degree. Sniff the wine, sip and keep it on your tongue, and let it play on your palate. Do not be in too much of a hurry to swallow the wine (which unless this is an official wine tasting will be the next step) but savour it; the aftertaste may be a delightful surprise, fruity, full-bodied and resonant. Other wines may leave a flat, harsh or indifferent aftertaste in the mouth. If you find a wine that pleases you, your enjoyment is the sole criterion. It goes without saying, I hope, that you will not smoke while tasting wine seriously.

Descriptive terms: favourable – robust, vigorous, rich, warm, full, elegant, velvety, soft, clean, tender; unfavourable – poor, thin, light, weak, sharp, unbalanced, heavy.

The alcoholic content of wines generally is favourably described as being lively, strong, generous, powerful, heady; unfavourably as harsh, insipid, sugary, acetic.

All wines have four components: acidity, tannin, fruit and alcohol content. Young wines have 'bite' – a combination of tannin and acid, expected but not excessive. 'Depth' implies a complex and desirable blend of lingering flavours in the aftertaste. A 'severe' wine has too much 'bite'. The 'finish' is good if the taste comes to a firm, crisp, pleasant conclusion. A poor finish is watery and unbalanced. Wine has 'potential' if too much tannin is present but the fruit is there 'Grip' is the point at which wine is balanced. After this point it eventually reaches a stage of development called 'going over the top' when it is no longer at its best because it is too old.

Let us look at two charts which show how red Bordeaux wines with a high

tannin content need time to get their grip, and how Beaujolais wines mature much younger because acidity predominates. Clarets take a long time to mature into big, sturdy wines, with surprising elegance, suppleness and finesse.

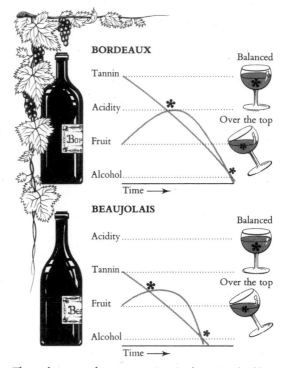

Those who want to learn to recognise wine by tasting should try to build up a memory bank of tastes.

In a Bordeaux, tannin predominates, then acid, then fruit, then alcohol content. As time goes on, the tannin level slowly sinks, the fruity quality develops, and these balance the acidity and alcohol, which remain constant. After a number of years the wine becomes 'balanced'. The fruitiness will increase for a time while the tannin declines steadily and then drops sharply, but at a certain point tannin and fruit sink to such an extent that the wine has 'gone over the top'. See how acidity predominates in a Beaujolais, and 'balance' is achieved earlier.

Recent vintage guide

	'66	'67	'68	'69	'70	'71	'72
Claret	7★	6	1	5★	7★	5★	–
Red Burgundy	6	4	1	7	5★	7★	–
White Burgundy	7	6	2	7	7	7	–
Sauternes	4	5	0	5	7	6	4
Loire	4	5	1	7	6	6	6
Rhône	6	6	2	5	5★	5★	5★
Rhine	6	5	3	6	5	7	1
Moselle	5	4	2	6	4	7	1
Champagne	7	–	–	–	–	–	–
Port	7★	7★	–	–	7★	–	–

7 = the best
0 = not recommended
★ Recommended for laying down.

How wine is made

All table wines, from the noblest to the least assuming, are made by fermenting some variety, or combination of varieties, of the grape species *Vitis vinifera*. It is further defined that the wine is made from fermented grape juice of freshly gathered grapes, and made in the district of origin of the grapes. The quality and flavour are affected by the geographical position, weather, soil and the varieties of grape. Each of the great vine-growing areas produces a number of varieties, sometimes as many as six. In Europe there are twenty-eight main varieties with names such as Riesling, Pinot Noir, Cabernet-Sauvignon, etc. Even the situation of a vineyard on a slope facing south may affect the quality of the wine produced there. Youthful strugglers to succeed in life often develop character while the spoiled darling of a rich family rarely amounts to anything. This is also true of wine. The soil that suits wine-producing vines best

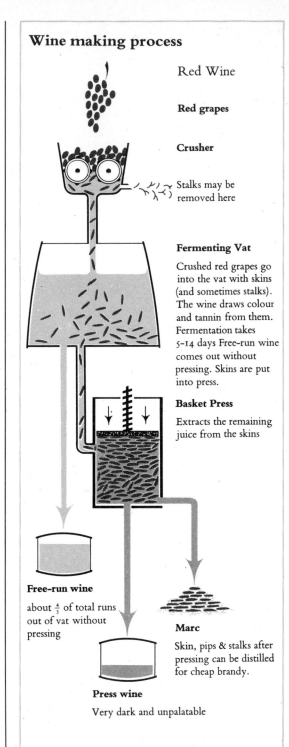

Wine making process

Red Wine

Red grapes

Crusher

Stalks may be removed here

Fermenting Vat

Crushed red grapes go into the vat with skins (and sometimes stalks). The wine draws colour and tannin from them. Fermentation takes 5-14 days Free-run wine comes out without pressing. Skins are put into press.

Basket Press

Extracts the remaining juice from the skins

Free-run wine

about ⅘ of total runs out of vat without pressing

Marc

Skin, pips & stalks after pressing can be distilled for cheap brandy.

Press wine

Very dark and unpalatable

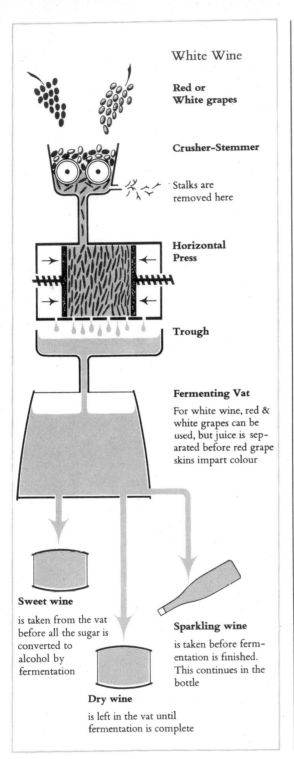

White Wine

Red or White grapes

Crusher-Stemmer

Stalks are removed here

Horizontal Press

Trough

Fermenting Vat

For white wine, red & white grapes can be used, but juice is separated before red grape skins impart colour

Sweet wine

is taken from the vat before all the sugar is converted to alcohol by fermentation

Sparkling wine

is taken before fermentation is finished. This continues in the bottle

Dry wine

is left in the vat until fermentation is complete

---

is normally low in humus and the finest wines come from areas where the weather is by no means reliable.

Grapes grown too far from the soil are too acid and have little flavour. The closer to the ground the better they mature, the sun's heat reflecting from the soil. In Madeira the grapes are grown on horizontal trellises, but in France and Germany the traditional method is usually seen – vines in straight lines a metre or so apart and severely pruned to leave a simple fruiting branch and another to put on wood for the next year.

At the time of the *vendange*, or grape harvest, the bunches of grapes are picked or cut by hand and taken to the fermenting vats. There they are fed into a crusher, sometimes with, sometimes without the stalks, and thence into fermenting vats. For white wines the grapes pass through a horizontal press first to remove the skins which would otherwise impart their colour. Either black or white grapes are used. The juice is then called 'must', and while fermentation progresses, sometimes for as long as two weeks, the yeasts either produce a dry wine by using up all the sugar in the 'must', or are killed off by the increasing proportion of alcohol, leaving some sugar unfermented and producing a sweet wine. Sparkling wines are fermented in the bottle – the *méthode champenoise* – or bottled before fermentation is complete. The *cuve close* method involves re-fermentation in pressurized tanks, bottling under pressure. A cheaper method is to inject carbon dioxide into the wine through the cork.

Grapes have a high sugar content, and natural yeasts and bacteria on the outer skin which cause fermentation. Special yeasts are now sometimes added to make up for nature's possible deficiencies and to ensure satisfactory fermentation. This yeast feeds upon the sugar, producing alcohol and carbonic acid gas which is given off in the form of bubbles. Fermentation is started by wild yeast, then taken over by wine yeasts.

Red wine: This is always made from black (or red) grapes. The wine draws both its purplish red colour and its tannin content from the skins and stalks. The wine is allowed to flow from the vat or *cuve* without pressing. All the residue is put into a basket press to extract the rest of the juice and this 'press wine' is dark and poor in flavour, but useful for blending. After this, the pressed skins, pips and stalks can be distilled to make *Marc*, a rough sort of brandy.

White wine: This may be made from black or white grapes, but the stalks and skins are always discarded before crushing. The harvest may be delayed until the grapes are partially dried, or infected with the 'noble rot', to obtain the characteristic bouquet and flavour of certain sweet white wines. From the crusher the grapes go straight into a horizontal press and the juice drips down into a trough which feeds the fermenting vat, thus discarding the skins before they colour the wine. Dry wines are fully fermented out.

The production of a stable sweet wine is not easy because the 'must' should have a higher sugar content so that sufficient alcohol is produced, say 14% (13% for Sauternes), leaving the desired amount of residual sugar, which might be as high as 20%.

The technical control of the natural processes varies, but might include racking off the yeast, or adding sulphur dioxide, or pasteurization.

Rosé wine: The process varies in different localities, but is usually the same as for red wine up to the point when it has had sufficient time in the fermenting vat to take on its characteristic pink colour from the skins. It then runs off into a second vat.

Perhaps the basic process is best described by a child who wrote as follows: 'When the grapes are all crushed up the yeast is hungry, and starts eating the sugar, and turns it into alcohol and gas, which in America is the same thing, but not here. When the yeast has eaten all the sugar, it dies of starvation, and what's left is wine.'

This is naturally an over-simplification since before delivery to your wine merchant in attractively labelled bottles wine may have gone through many other processes, including racking, fining and the onslaught and cure of certain diseases which young wines, like young children, are subject to. For wine enthusiasts these processes are fully explained in books referred to in our bibliography.

Glossary of terms

It is annoying to be at a loss when a term you hear mentioned or read on a label is a bit of a mystery. But it is all part of your wineupmanship to understand what these terms mean and the following glossary sheds light on those which have not been more fully explained elsewhere in this chapter.

Bodega – Spanish for cellar or store.

Bottle sickness – a passing distemper which affects some still wines when they are bottled; it is caused by deprivation of oxygen, but rights itself if left alone.

Bouchonné – French term for 'corked', used of wine that has been spoiled by a defective cork.

Brut – an unsweetened wine.

Cabernet – Kabinett – special wines to be kept in the 'cupboard' for the host and his guests. Also family name of a variety of black grapes.

Capsule – cap used to protect the surface of corks exposed to the air and usually designed to improve the appearance.

Cassis – a confusing term as it applies to a wine of the Côtes de Provence; a blackcurrant liqueur; a non-alcoholic cordial.

Cellar – a place suitable for storage of bottled wine where the temperature remains reasonably low and constant. In French *cave*, in German *Keller*.

Chambré – refers to red wine which has been brought to room temperature.

Chaptalisé – French term applied to wine in which the alcoholic strength has been raised by adding extra sugar.

Château – the 'house' of a wine producing estate, not necessarily a castle.

Château bottled – a wine bottled where it was made, recorded on labels as *Mise en bouteille au Château* or *Mise du Château*.

Claret – French red wine from the Bordeaux district, the term being derived from *clairet* or *clairette*, a wine made from a blend of black and white grapes.

Clos – a descriptive term of a vineyard which has at one time been fully enclosed, usually by a wall or fence.

Commune – a group of vineyards in one parish.

Consume – Portuguese *vin ordinaire*.

Corky or *corked* – wine tainted by a dirty or diseased cork.

Coupage – blending of wines.

Cru – a vineyard or vineyards producing wines of the same quality and standard. The 'growth' or wine produced by a particular vineyard. In the Bordeaux area the finest wines were described as *grand cru*, *premier cru*, *premier grand cru*, descending in order to the *cinquième cru*.

Crust – sediment thrown by red wine in the bottle.

Cuvée – may mean merely blending but in Burgundy *Tête de Cuvée* and in Champagne *Première Cuvée* indicate first and superior pressings.

Cuve Close – a closed tank for the production of sparkling wines.

Domaine – the equivalent of Château in some areas of France, principally in the Bourgogne, or area surrounding a château as in *Domaines du Château de* . . .

Fermentation – the wine making process by which sugar is converted by yeast into alcohol and carbon dioxide.

Fiasco – Italian word for flask usually referring to round straw-covered bottle.

Finings – purifiers of wine which sink slowly clearing all the sedimentation.

Fine – cheap brandy.

Goût – French word for taste. *Déguster* means to taste and enjoy.

Goutte, vin de – the earlier pressings which go to make the finest wines.

Grande Marque – French term referring to the best known names in champagne.

Heel – a very small amount of wine remaining in a bottle which has not been poured off because of the sediment.

Hock – Anglicised abbreviation of Hochheimer loosely applied since Victorian days to all light white sparkling German wines.

Konsumwein – German equivalent of vin ordinaire.

Lees – deposits of sediment remaining in the bottom of a wine cask or bottle.

Leger – French term for wine of low alcoholic strength.

Maderisation – oxidation and consequent discoloration.

Maturation – a process whereby the main elements (tannin, acid, sugar, alcohol) combine over a period of time.

Moscatel – Spanish term for sweet white wine made from muscat grapes. A French white wine made from these grapes is called *Muscat*, an Italian wine *Moscatello* or *Moscato*.

Nature – French term for unsweetened Champagne. German terms Natur, Naturrein, Naturwein, all relate to wines naturally fermented without added sugar.

Non-vintage – describes a blend of wines made from grapes gathered in different years, to achieve a consistent quality.

Phylloxera – the insect pest which in the 1860s to 1890s destroyed most of the vines in Europe. Today, all European vines are grafted to American root stock which is resistant to the insect. Ironically, the insect comes from America.

Punt – term used to describe the hollow in the bottom of various wine bottles.

Quinta – Portuguese wine estate.

Rendement – the amount of wine allowed to be produced by a vineyard.

Schloss – German for castle or estate.

Sommelier – French for wine waiter.

Ullage – a bottle with a faulty cork which has allowed some of the wine to escape. Ullaged claret or Burgundy is always spoilt, but ullaged champagne may be excellent. Ullage also refers to a cask of wine no longer full to the bung.

Vignoble – the vineyard where the grapes are grown. Although the location, nature of the soil and climate all affect individual vineyards, poor soil usually produces the best wine.

Vigneron – the man responsible for growing and harvesting the grapes.

Vin de garde – wine suitable for laying down.

Vin de paille – sweet wine made from very ripe grapes left in the sun on straw mats after picking.

Vin ordinaire – also called *vin de con-*sommation; a blended wine under a brand name, for daily consumption.

Vinification – the system employed in making wine.

Vintage – the time when grapes are gathered; if followed by a date, signifies the wine is made from grapes gathered in that year, from a single harvest. In hot countries where the weather varies little from one year to another, vintages are less important.

Viticulture – growing grapes.

Weeper – bottle showing the first signs of a defective cork; it should be drunk before it becomes an ullage, or recorked, which is less satisfactory.

Breaking the ice abroad

How to say 'cheers' and offer a drink to foreigners who, poor devils, cannot understand English.

French: A votre santé. Permettez-moi de vous offrir un verre!

Italian: La sua saluta. Oche cosa desidera?

German: Prosit. Was trinken Sie? (Or, more formally) Darf ich Ihnen ein Glass anbieten?

Spanish: ¡Salud! ¿Que quiere tomar?

Dutch: Proost. Kan ik u een drankje aanbieden?

Note: Skol says cheers in all Scandinavian languages, so remember you can greet the entire company by raising your glass, looking all round and murmuring 'rund skol' before drinking, but to be polite you *must* catch everyone's eye. Danes particularly spend a great deal of their time doing this.

Descriptive terms in foreign languages

French: *brut* – extra dry, *sec* – dry, *demi-sec* – medium sweet, *doux* – sweet, *blanc* – white, *rouge* – red, *rosé* – pink, *mousseux* – sparkling, *pétillant* – semi-sparkling.

Italian: *secco* – dry, *abboccato* – sweet, *bianco* – white, *rosso* – red, *rosato* – pink, *spumante* – sparkling, *frizzante* – semi-sparkling.

German: *trocken* – dry, *süss* – sweet, *weiss* – white, *rot* – red, *rosé* – pink, *sekt* – champagne, *schaumwein* – sparkling, *spritzig* – semi-sparkling.

Spanish: *seco* – dry, *dulce* – sweet, *bianco* – white, *tinto* – red, *rosado* – pink, *espumoso* – sparkling, *semi-espumoso* – semi-sparkling.

Finding a home for your wines

A wine cellar need not be underground. Indeed, in a modern house or flat how many people these days have a real cellar? Find a corner which is clean, adequately ventilated, not damp, removed from the vicinity of hot water pipes and boilers and reasonably dark. Wines like peace, quiet and very little light. For this reason, the wines most easily damaged by exposure to strong light are bottled in dark green or brown glass. Your wine racks could be in a small box room, or a cupboard in a larger room, or under the stairs, provided the site is not subject to extremes of temperature, or expected to house un-welcome neighbours such as strong smelling cans of paraffin. Because of the polluted atmosphere a garage, otherwise an obvious choice well out of harm's way, might be totally unsuitable. Dampness might encourage cork weevils, which would eat through the corks, or cause moulds to form and spoil the labels.

Wines should be handled gently at all times, and stored horizontally in racks (with the labels uppermost), so that the wine is in contact with the cork. If the bottle is left standing upright for any length of time (longer than six months) the cork dries out and shrinks, and allows air to get into the bottle and evaporate the wine.

The ideal storage conditions

It may not be possible to provide the constant temperature conditions your wine merchant would recommend, but if the range is between 55°F and 60°F (13°C and 16°C) he would approve. With modern central heating reaching every corner of the house, the storage temperature may be well above the ideal winter and summer temperatures, and discourage you from laying down wine for the future; in fact wine is little affected by being stored at a consistently high temperature, and though it dislikes undue heat, such as the proximity of a radiator, that is better than allowing the temperature to sink perilously near freezing point. It is the steadiness of the temperature that matters, even if it is always approaching 70°F in your home.

It may seem obvious to remark that other foods or fuels with a strong smell should not be kept in the same room, but it might not cross your mind that you could also harm wine by storing it where there is any considerable traffic vibration, or, if you live in a block of flats, in a store-room directly under the lift shaft.

Permanent racking can be built up in matching units of twelve or more open-ings and I prefer those with wood and metal struts. However, a twelve-bottle cardboard carton, standing on its side, makes a temporary bin or rack. Occasionally wines begin to ooze out through the cork, so watch for this symptom and use up the bottle quickly. Although all bottles should be stored horizontally, red wines ought to stand upright at least twenty-four hours before opening to allow the sediment to settle, and with older and finer wines with more sediment, twice as long. This is the great advantage of keeping a small stock at home. Wine needs to rest after a journey or, like a tired traveller, it becomes irritable and does not give its best. If you bring in a supply as little as two days before you open and serve the first bottle (leaving the reds for immediate use upright and not on their sides), these bottles will be in better condition than a couple you dash out to buy on impulse or through necessity just before a meal.

Preparing wines for the table

Stand *all* the bottles you intend to serve upright beforehand. This is particularly important for red wines as it allows the sediment to settle, but white wines also sometimes cast off a sediment unless matured in the cask, carefully racked and bottled or filtered – a procedure which ensures brightness, though it may do so to the detriment of the bouquet. Experts like to move their stately Burgundies into the room in which they will be served two days in advance. Young red wines which throw little sediment should still stand upright for a day if you can arrange it. This advice is a counsel of perfection and may be unrealistic; it may be necessary to speed up the raising of temperature. Such expedients as standing it near a fire or plunging the bottle into hot water, etc., are harmful and almost too painful to mention, but might be unavoidable.

Decanting helps to avoid sediment in the glass when an older wine has not had long enough in the upright position to settle, and improves young wines noticeably simply by aeration and by dispersing any unpleasant smell from the bottle. A tip on decanting, which raises the temperature quickly, is to heat a carafe by pouring hot water over the sides, and then to decant the wine into it. A decanter (which might not stand this rough treatment) usually has a stopper, and for more mature wines, this should be replaced. A young wine in the carafe, with no stopper, would benefit from much longer opportunity to 'breathe', two hours for a sturdy young Beaujolais or up to four hours for the less familiar red wines of the Languedoc, Corbières and Minervois. The carafe or decanter can then stand happily in the airing cupboard. Don't forget that wine glasses can be cradled in the hand to warm the contents; an overheated wine is ruined.

Make sure your wines are at the right temperature before uncorking. White and rosé wines are served cool but not iced; say between 45° and 55°F for dry wines and between 40° and 45°F for sweet ones. Two hours in the refrigerator door or one hour at the most in the refrigerator cabinet should be enough, but avoid placing bottles in the freezer even for a short time. Wrapping in a napkin wrung out in cold water helps, but plays havoc with the label, and putting outside the window in winter is distinctly hazardous. Alternatively, wrap the bottle in a few sheets of newspaper and put it in the refrigerator cabinet for four hours. This helps the wine to cool evenly and slowly.

Sparkling wines, especially Champagnes, are served slightly chilled, preferably from an ice bucket. If you cannot improvise one, use the refrigerator cabinet, increasing the time allowed. For *al fresco* eating, bottles can be transported wrapped in a layer of wet newspaper or a wet towel, then protected by a plastic bag, at the last moment before leaving the house. If the picnic site is near flowing water, tie a piece of string firmly round the neck of each bottle. They can then be anchored and gently submerged in water for half an hour on arrival. White and rosé wines are less temperamental travellers than red wines so are naturally the best choice for a picnic.

Over-chilling of white wines removes the 'nose', and deprives us of the anticipatory pleasure of enjoying the bouquet. Hasty chilling by putting ice into the wine itself (unless it is a mixed drink such as a cold cup) is definitely bad form because it insults the wine. The melting ice soon dilutes it to a beverage suitable only for children, and it is not much liked by them once they are over the age of three.

Red wines are served *chambrés*, that is at the temperature of a room which is comfortably warm but not hot, say between 60° and 65°F.

The opening ceremony

Let's begin with sparkling wines where no corkscrew is required, and once the restraining wire is removed, the cork may be forced out violently by the carbon dioxide in the wine itself. To open champagne, or any other sparkling wine, the bottle, duly chilled, should be swathed in a clean napkin, and the cork pointed at the least vulnerable target; not your own or a visitor's eye for instance, nor a window. Remove the wire muzzle, holding the cork down, and turn the bottle, rather than *vice versa*. Pull the cork out slowly as you turn! Have an assistant with several glasses at the ready, and you may be able to pour a half-inch into each, without any overspill, topping up these glasses as the bubbles subside.

White and rosé wines do not require to be opened and allowed to 'breathe' as red wines do before serving. Providing they are properly cooled they can be served within minutes of drawing the cork. Red wines, however, require much more careful treatment, partly to avoid disturbing the sediment and partly because all red wines, especially the younger and bolder ones, acquire a much greater maturity and roundness by exposure to the air at the right temperature after opening.

Treat all semi-sparkling and still whites and rosés in the same way; feel the bottle to make sure it is just sufficiently cool, remove the capsule, draw the cork, wipe the neck, and pour. Try to keep the bottle cool until it is empty, as these wines lose all their character if served lukewarm after being in a warm room.

Red wines require to stand long enough to allow them to come up to room temperature. A fine wine will not need to be uncorked more than an hour before the meal. An old and honoured vintage might require only a few minutes, especially if it is a Burgundy. Young (and thankfully cheaper) red wines benefit from a minimum of two hours breathing space.

Decanting stops sediment from reaching the glass and is, to my mind, an agreeable preliminary to the pleasure of drinking the wine. Remove the capsule, uncork the bottle, wipe the neck inside and out with a napkin, and have ready a warm, dry decanter or carafe. Place a light behind the bottle, about four inches to the right of the decanter (or the left if you are left handed), at a height which brings it

29

directly behind the neck of the bottle as you pour. A candle in a fairly tall candlestick is ideal. It does not have to be a candle, although the French term for decanting is *à la bougie*. A smallish table lamp with the shade removed is suitable if less romantic. As you pour the wine steadily with the light directly behind the neck of the bottle, you can see when the sediment reaches it and cease decanting. Do not turn the bottle upwards to see how much is left once you have started pouring, as this creates a vacuum and disturbs the sediment. Stop in good time. The lees in the bottle, if strained through muslin, a clean white handkerchief or filter papers obtainable from wine merchants can be used for cooking. Replace the stopper in the decanter unless the wine requires further aeration. Younger wines rarely have sufficient sedimentation to need decanting, other than for warming and aerating.

By the way, keep the bottle on show. Guests are interested to know what they are drinking, and sometimes may be faintly suspicious that you have decanted a wine you are not proud to offer.

White wines also throw some sediment unless carefully racked and bottled. It is a pity to strain it, since this removes a certain amount of flavour. The sediment does no harm, but it does not look good in the glass. This is undoubtedly why white wines were so often served in coloured or Venetian glasses as a disguise.

Port, especially old port, may be more difficult to decant. First of all the cork may not come out in one piece as the wine may have rotted it. If it breaks, get out as much as you can and strain the port through muslin or a fine tea strainer. You may notice a substance called beeswing on the top of the port; this is harmless and is formed from living organisms which help make a vintage wine the delight it is.

Corkscrews and cradles

I agree that wines are like babies and need nursing, but a cradle is going too far.

Cradles are definitely not necessary, in fact, not favoured by experts, since they keep the wine at an angle where the sediment is likely to be disturbed as you pour. Wine experts prefer red wines to be decanted rather than cradled in a basket. Never put a cradle on the table, unless it was a present from one of your guests.

A good strong corkscrew is essential and easier to use than a cheap or delicate one. Remove the capsule first with a knife. Insert the tip of the corkscrew in the centre of the cork and screw down vertically, so that it does not emerge halfway down the neck at the side, and split the cork when pressure is applied to draw it. If a second attempt damages the cork seriously, the only course left may be to push the cork in and strain the wine from the bottle into a carafe through muslin – a desperate solution only to be attempted if driven demented by thirst, and this the only bottle in the house. The kind of corkscrew amateurs have most success with is a

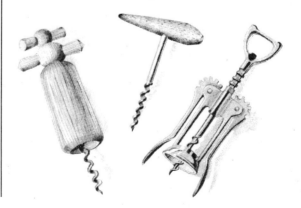

double lever bell type or the metal cantilever. Both types fit over the neck of the bottle and ensure that the screw enters the cork in the centre and exert an even, effortless 'pull'. The injection type sometimes works and sometimes does not.

Pouring with panache

Do not over-fill wine glasses. The glass is intended to offer you a chance to appreciate the aroma before you sip, and short of dipping your nose into liquid this is not possible if the glass is filled to brimming point. At least an inch of space should be left to ensure that the aroma is trapped and can be channelled to the nose. The suggestion that a host is ungenerous if he fills your glass only two-thirds full is absurd; equally unflattering to his guests is the impression that he is trying to divide the wine equally among them, and be done with it. A half-filled glass offered for your consideration and comment is far more of a compliment.

The choice of glasses

The classic shapes have all evolved because they suit the wines for which they are intended. The short-stemmed goblet is intended for red wines, so that your hand can naturally encircle the glass, warm it further if necessary by keeping it there, and bring it to your lips. Glasses should never be too thick, for this reason.

Long-stemmed glasses are intended for white wine, so that the hand only touches the stem, and does not inadvertently warm the wine. There are some with especially long stems intended for white wines from Alsace and the Rhine. The traditional Bordeaux glass, also used for Beaujolais and other red wines generally, is less wide and more tulip shaped than a Burgundy glass. A Champagne glass should be a tulip or flute shape; the very open coupe shape allows the sparkle to disappear too rapidly. It is better to conserve it rather than attempt to revive it with that inane toy, the swizzle stick, or clutch it firmly so that it quickly loses its chill.

For a meal with several wines, provide one glass for dry white wines, one glass for red wines, one glass for sweet white wines, and one for sparkling wines. This advice applies more to formal banquets rather than to home entertaining. If the choice offered is to be dry white followed by red, possibly ending with a sweet white with dessert, set the glasses on the right of each table setting, near to hand in the sequence they are to be used.

In order not to confuse the palate it is customary to serve light, delicate wines first; then full-bodied ones. White wines come before reds except for sweet dessert ones, or Champagne, or some other white sparkling wine, to end the meal. Always serve light before heavy and young before old wines.

Cognac is served in France in a small tulip shaped glass, and Armagnac, the oldest and proudest of French brandies, in a larger rounder glass. The pretentions of serving anything in an enormous balloon glass, warmed over a spirit warmer, is one I have yet to encounter in the French home. Liqueurs require tiny glasses in which they will not be lost, the most usual shape being like a miniature Bordeaux glass. It is an understandable mistake if one has no liqueur glasses to offer too much, since the customary two tablespoons only seems adequate in a proportionate glass. Port and sherry glasses come in various shapes, all smaller in capacity than wine glasses, but the copita or tulip shape, the traditional sherry taster's glass, is now accepted as the best glass for sherry.

Ordering wine in a restaurant

Nothing embarrasses the host or hostess of a party dining out more than making a mess of ordering the wine. If hitherto familiar names in clarets and Burgundies appear astonishingly costly on the wine list, and other names meaningless, here is how to cope. In a first class restaurant you may be offered a wine list with the Cellar Master's selection on a separate sheet in front. These will be medium priced to expensive wines, expertly chosen and excellent value. If all are beyond your means, glance through the wine list, and unless a wine to suit your pocket and the dishes chosen by your guests catches your eye, enlist the advice of the wine waiter, who may also be called the wine butler or *sommelier*. Point to a wine at about the price you intend to pay, and say (if for instance you are eating fish) 'We're having the sole, do you recommend this, or something dryer?' If he is worthy of his profession, he will perhaps improve on your choice but not suggest a wine costing double. If he does, make a mental note not to patronize the place again.

Wine *en carafe* can be a disaster, partly because there are no laws on quantity in Britain, partly because of ignorance on the part of the management. Most restaurants, however, now serve the same reliable *vins ordinaires* available in litre and larger sizes from the wine merchant. Properly presented, they are marvellously drinkable, and if you get red ink or paint stripper send it back. Make sure you taste a little quickly, before it is poured for the whole party as your point, if you want to

complain, is stronger if only one sip of the wine has been consumed. A corky wine will leave an extremely unpleasant after-taste, and the whole bin may be affected. Consult the wine waiter and choose something different.

Quality may be a question of debate, but as far as quantity is concerned, a carafe should hold 24 fluid oz., a half carafe 12 fluid oz., and wine bought by the glass should be served in a 5 oz. Paris goblet – which means that allowing for serving space at the top, six such glasses equal a carafe.

More worthwhile tips for the wine lover; if you order a bottle of red, it may be *chambré*, but it will not yet have been opened and had time to breathe. Decide, order, and make sure that the bottle is opened at once and placed on your table if it needs contact with the air, while the food is being prepared.

Restaurants which serve red wine in a cradle often do this because the sediment has not had time to settle, and the tilting of the bottle helps this. But the last two glasses from the bottle may be cloudy and far from perfect.

If you order white wine, you have to guard against being served a wine that is not cold enough. Feel the bottle first to make sure the claim that it is already chilled is true. If not, ask for it to be put in an ice bucket on or near your table for a few minutes, and do not let an over-enthusiastic waiter pour half of it out, warm, into the glasses, before you can stop him.

Wine traps for the unwary

It is a source of embarrassment to the uninitiated that so many important reds begin with the letter B. The clarets are

Salade Côte d'Azur

Bordeaux wines, those subtle, fine and elegant wines with which we have long had a national affinity. They should not be confused with the soft, fruity Beaujolais, lighthearted and intended to be drunk *young*, from the southern part of Bourgogne. The true Burgundies are rough when drunk young, but mature to a velvety glowing distinction which makes Burgundy 'the King of wines'.

Wines meant to be drunk young are fermented for a very short time only. By far the best known is the 'Beaujolais Nouveau'. The vintage takes place on 9th September, and the wine is ready to travel by 16th November. There is quite a race to be the first to get it to Britain each year. It is delicious cool, but not chilled, and is slightly *pétillant*. It is at its best around Christmas and should all be finished by the middle of March. If you take a winter skiing holiday, look out for the Swiss equivalent *Sauser*, and in Austria, *Heurige*. It is reasonably cheap and pleasant.

The unidentical twins

Understandably, Pouilly Fuissé and Pouilly Fumé are thought to come from the same area of France, and to be in the same sort of relationship as spätlese and auslese. The first of these two wines is in fact a white Burgundy, produced in the environs of the two villages, Pouilly and Fuissé, whereas Pouilly Fumé comes from the Loire and has a pronounced smoky flavour.

Another puzzler for amateurs of wine appreciation is the difference between Moselles and Rhine wines. A great deal of the Moselle river runs through France, and the wines of this area are French. However, it suddenly decides not to run into the North Sea, but turns away to meet the Rhine near its source, and we come to the German Rhine wines. Moselles are usually bottled in dark green glass, and Rhine wines in dark brown; an easy aid to distinction, since all the names *sound* German. To those who wonder why we associate the name of Hock with Victoriana, the answer is that as we adapted the name Claret from the French in mediaeval times, and Rhenish from the German *Rheinisch*, we decided that Hochheimer being a fair example of all Rhine wines with names ticklish to pronounce, all wines from that area would henceforth be called Hock. Queen Victoria pronounced it the best of the German wines. We have taken similar liberties with port (from Portugal) and sherry (a misspelling of Jerez). Moselles are greenish in colour, very light, delicate in bouquet, and perhaps rather lacking in body, not surprisingly, since the soil which nourishes the grape is poor and stony and the vines have a constant battle to survive. Rhine wines, nourished by richer soil, which we call Hocks, are more powerful, deeper in colour, more developed in maturity and dignity.

The marriage of wine with food

As every matchmaker knows, one sometimes misjudges affinities. What may be classically acceptable, or your own personal choice, may not please someone else. There will always be people who prefer red wine with fish, and would rather have a sweet Sauternes with their cheese than a majestic Burgundy. This guide therefore is in the most general terms, and where I have my own bias towards a particular wine with a certain dish, I have indicated it under the 'take a leaf' symbol on the appropriate page.

With clear soup: Dry sherry with game or meat soup, or consommé; Madeira with turtle soup.

With shellfish and fish: Dry white wines, especially Chablis, those of the Loire, Moselle and Rhine. Also dry white sparkling wines, including Champagne *brut*.

With hors d'oeuvre, light entrées and white meats: Dry or medium dry white wines and rosés, and semi-sparkling wines; especially Portuguese vinhos verdes and rosés, Italian Soave and Orvieto Abboccato.

With meat and poultry: Light to medium heavy red wines, especially those of Bordeaux and Beaujolais.

With game, rich meat dishes: The great red wines, especially Burgundy.

With cheese: Robust red wines of good vintages for preference with strong cheeses; regional white wines with mild cheeses; port with blue cheeses and nuts.

With pâté de foie gras, other pâtés and terrines: Light or full-bodied vintage red wine, or sweet white wine, especially Barsac and Sauternes.

With sweets: Champagne *demi-sec*, other sparkling and sweet semi-sparkling wines, especially Tokay.

With fruit: Sweet white wines, Champagne *demi-sec* or Vouvray. With crisp, slightly acid fruit such as apples, no wine marries well. As the professionals say, 'Buy on an apple and sell on cheese'.

Apéritifs: Pale and medium sherry, dry Madeira, Vermouths, Champagne *brut*. Gin and vodka based cocktails tend to confuse the palate and deaden the appetite.

Conserving leftover wine for cooking

Wine, once it is opened and exposed to the air, begins to alter. Spirits and liqueurs should be kept securely corked to prevent evaporation, but alter very little. Fortified wines (and this also includes vermouths and branded apéritifs) should be stored upright in a cool place, and will not deteriorate for several months. Light sherries and dry vermouths are the earliest to suffer. Table wines, however, cannot stand exposure for long, so once opened treat them with great care.

It is better to transfer to a smaller bottle to protect the wine from oxidation by air (I keep a few half bottles with plastic stoppers handy, for this purpose), and white wine thus rebottled keeps well if stored in a cool place for one or two days. Red wines ought not to be kept cool, but left at the temperature they were served at and rebottled with a spoonful of port, sherry or brandy. If you have no possibility or wish to use up table wines for drinking, use them for cooking. It will be a week or more before the taste verges on vinegar for cooking purposes. More joy is yet in store for freezer owners. Small amounts of wine can be frozen successfully in wide-necked containers – little polythene ones with snap-on seals, or glass jars, for instance. Do not use bottles with a narrow neck, or the wine, with its high water content, may burst the neck as it expands rapidly up the narrow space on freezing, so allow a reasonable headspace, usually reckoned to be one-tenth of the height of the container.

Mixing your Drinks

All of us who frequently imbibe alcohol find the path to pleasure a joy, but the return journey is sometimes rough. For wine lovers, a hard head is not as important as a sensitive palate, but for those who mix their drinks, or even drink table wines in considerable quantities, the following hints may be useful.

How to drink without getting drunk

The best way of all is to drink while you are eating. Food does not prevent your system from absorbing alcohol, but it slows down the process, and since, literally, time spent eating is not time spent drinking, it limits your intake during any given space of time. If attending a 'drinks only' party where the most substantial item on offer is likely to be a salted nut or crisp, many people believe in lining the stomach beforehand with some fatty food to ward off the immediate impact of alcohol. Try swallowing a glass of milk, or a tablespoon of olive oil just before joining the party, by all means. A nice padding of mashed potato (with salt, pepper and nutmeg, why not?) has been found effective, or a couple of tablespoons of honey is another alternative, actually endorsed by the medical profession. Fruit, or anything containing vitamin C, for some reason absorbs alcohol. But eventually the alcohol will break down these defences and lay you flat, if drunk in sufficiently large quantities. Oddly enough, this also works in reverse. Very rich and oily food which produces a queasy sensation (especially if consumed in a hot or inadequately ventilated room) calls for a quick gulp of brandy, taken neat, and this often enables you to proceed triumphantly to the sweet course and cheese. Dilution is another form of defence. Long drinks take longer to drink, and in the course of an evening you will not actually have consumed so much alcohol; better still, occasionally have a long drink where gin or vodka might be concealed but is in fact omitted. The half-and-half tipple rushes straight into your bloodstream, as whisky and water drinkers know to their cost.

The great thing is to be relaxed, and if possible static, while drinking, and to take it slowly. If you are tired, forced to chat, to stand up, or even to dance, for hours on end, and at the same time drink as fast as a waiter can be persuaded to refill your glass, you have a greater chance of ending up drunk than if you consumed the same amount of alcohol during a leisurely dinner party.

Mixed drinks have the unsavoury reputation of making you drunker than if you stuck to the grain or the grape (i.e. whisky with beer chasers although there is a saying 'Whisky after beer, never fear, beer after whisky, very risky'; or sherry followed by table wines, port or brandy). Friends who have put this to the test disagree as to whether there is any truth in it.

For timid drinkers who find it hard to refuse, but also hard to take, some drinks last a long time and have little kick, without advertising the weak head. It is smart to ask for tomato juice and make believe it's a Bloody Mary, very chic to drink

Riesling and soda, the modern version of hock and seltzer; and quite effective for women (who are supposed to enjoy liqueurs at any time of the day or night) to ask for a fruit liqueur on the rocks! Poured over crushed ice, like the Italian *Granita di caffé* or *di limone*, it looks pretty and does little harm. If you know in advance, or hope the evening is likely to lead to serious drinking, put a measured amount of water in a glass and an antacid tablet side by side on your bedside table and swallow the mixture before you go to sleep. The odds are you will be in no condition to think of searching for the remedy then. At least drink a glass or more of water before you turn in.

How to deal with a hangover

We now take up where we left off. The tablet you forgot to take last night may assuage the worst pangs. By the way, bicarbonate of soda is too powerful, leave it where it belongs in the kitchen for cooking and burns. Drinking a lot of water is a physical necessity; since alcohol dehydrates the system, drink as much as you can. 'Morning after' fizzing remedies that contain aspirin might be dangerous to the health; effervescent tablets containing ascorbic acid are safer, better for you and taste much nicer. A glass of cold milk works wonders (if you like milk). If you must fortify yourself against the new day, sugary black coffee (if your weight allows it) consumed with bread, very little butter and a lot of honey, would be reasonable. A Prairie Oyster has never been known to help, so I do not give the recipe; it merely indicates that you are sufficiently in command of yourself to swallow a raw egg. The hair of the dog, taken about the middle of the morning, reassures those who woke up swearing they will never touch alcohol again.

A sideways glance at cocktails

This section does not really include cocktails, but as Dry Martinis are particularly popular, here is the recipe. Fill a large jug three-quarters full with ice, pour in twelve parts gin to one part dry vermouth, stir well with a long-handled spoon, allow to stand for only one or two minutes to make the mixture cold, but do not let the ice melt enough to dilute it seriously. Have ready a saucer full of slivers of lemon zest (peel thinly, leaving the white pith behind). Put a sliver in each glass and strain over them the chilled gin and vermouth mixture. Don't mix just one and put a lump of ice into the warm mixture; it doesn't taste the same and no-one will thank you for it.

Vodka is growing apace in popularity. Tomato juice with vodka and ice (a measure of vodka to about 7 tablespoons tomato juice packs a wallop for the unwary) but it needs a touch of lemon juice and Worcestershire sauce to make it taste like a non-alcoholic drink, if that is what you want. A Vodkatini, equal quantities of vodka and dry Martini on the rocks, tastes as lyrical as it sounds. A Green Dragon tastes more friendly than you might expect, but it does have a bit of a fiery breath. It is made with equal parts of vodka and crème de menthe shaken with crushed ice.

These, however, are rather outside our scope, so with a passing reference to Pink Gin, which is just ice, a few drops of Angostura bitters and gin, and is much more palatable diluted with Perrier than soda water, let us pass on to mixed drinks of which wine is the basic element. As a rough guide to expenditure, the recipes tend to rise in price as they do in elegance and alcoholic content. But since the usual aim when entertaining is to promote mild merriment rather than a bacchanalian orgy, do not pass over cheaper ones as being beneath your notice. All these bowls, cups and punches are a little different from the usual recipes. None are given later in the special section on parties.

Syrup for punches and cups

8 oz sugar
5 fl oz water

Dissolve the sugar in the water over low heat. When completely dissolved, bring to the boil and boil vigorously for 2 minutes. Cool and use as required. If, for example, the recipe calls for 4 oz sugar, add half the syrup. It keeps well in a polythene container in the refrigerator for up to a week.

Orange fire punch

$6\frac{1}{4}$ fl oz can frozen orange concentrate
25 fl oz water
5 fl oz pineapple juice
3 tablespoons lemon juice
1 small bottle tonic water
2–3 tablespoons Cointreau
ice cubes

Mix together the orange juice, water, pineapple juice and lemon juice and chill thoroughly. Pour into a punch bowl and just before serving stir in the tonic water, liqueur and ice cubes.

Sangria bianca

2 peaches
1 orange, sliced
1 lemon, sliced
1 tablespoon sugar
1 inch cinnamon stick
1 litre white vin ordinaire
1 litre rosé vin ordinaire
1 large bottle fizzy lemonade

Peel, stone and slice the peaches and put into a large punch bowl with the orange and lemon slices. Add the sugar, cinnamon and wine and stir well. Leave to stand for an hour. Remove cinnamon stick and add chilled lemonade just before serving.

Douro punch

1 small fresh pineapple
1 bottle tawny port
1 litre red vin ordinaire
4 oz sugar
2 bottles sparkling cider de luxe
cucumber slices to decorate

Peel the pineapple, remove hard core and cut flesh into wedges. Place these in a large punch bowl and pour over the port, wine and sprinkle in the sugar. Stir well and chill. Just before serving add the cider and float cucumber slices on the top.

Ananaspunsch

8 oz can sliced pineapple
7 tablespoons Madeira
2 oz sugar
10 fl oz hot strong tea, strained
juice of 1 lemon
1 litre red vin ordinaire
5 fl oz Pernod

Put the drained pineapple slices into a punch bowl, pour over a little syrup from the can and the Madeira and allow to stand for 2 hours. Dissolve the sugar in the hot tea, add the lemon juice and wine and heat to just below boiling point. Pour over the pineapple and finally stir in the Pernod.

Tournament cup

8 oz strawberries, sliced
1 litre light red wine
5 fl oz brandy
2 large bottles fizzy lemonade
1 lemon, sliced to decorate

Place the strawberries in the base of a punch bowl and pour over the brandy and wine. Allow to stand for at least an hour. Just before serving add the lemonade and float the lemon slices on the top.

Frosty Christmas cup

3 oz sugar
5 fl oz water
2 sticks cinnamon
2 lemons
2 oranges
ice
2 litres rosé vin ordinaire
soda water
orange and lemon slices to decorate

Bring the sugar and water slowly to the boil. Add the cinnamon sticks, simmer for 5 minutes, then remove them. Squeeze juice from fruit, add to the syrup and cool. Put a large block of ice in a bowl, pour over the syrup, add the wine and dilute with soda water to taste. Serve with orange and lemon slices floating on top.

Excelsior

3 egg yolks
4 oz sugar
1 tumbler crushed ice
1 tumbler fresh orange juice
2 tablespoons Cointreau
4 tablespoons brandy
1 bottle dry sparkling white wine

Beat the egg yolks and sugar together in a large bowl until pale and foamy. Add the crushed ice, orange juice, liqueur and brandy. Stir well but quickly. Pour in the wine and serve at once in tumblers.

Taunton punch

10 fl oz dry sherry
1 bottle stout
1 bottle lager
1 flagon medium sweet cider
ice cubes
lemon slices to decorate

Put sherry, stout, lager and half the cider into a punch bowl and chill. Just before serving add the remaining cider, the ice cubes and lemon slices.

Bière au citron

for each person:
1 teaspoon sugar
½ teaspoon lemon juice
1 tablespoon brandy
1 small bottle pale ale
pinch grated nutmeg

Put the sugar, lemon juice and brandy into a chilled glass. Pour in the chilled ale, giving it a good head, and sprinkle with grated nutmeg.

Whisky sour

for each person:
1 teaspoon sugar
1–2 tablespoons lemon juice
1 measure whisky
½ tumbler crushed ice

Stir the sugar into the lemon juice. Add the whisky and pour over the ice. This looks and tastes nice decorated with a slice of orange and a slice of lemon.

Brandy frost

Dip the rim of each glass in orange juice then into caster sugar to coat the rim evenly. Put three parts brandy, one part Cointreau and three parts orange juice into a shaker. Add three parts ice and shake well. Pour carefully into the glasses.

Le Kir

Pour some liqueur de cassis into a glass and add to it chilled white Burgundy or any other chilled dry white wine (about one part liqueur to six parts wine). This drink is a firm favourite in Dijon, where every café serves it.

Black velvet

Traditionally made by pouring equal parts of stout and champagne into a tumbler half-filled with crushed ice.

When funds are low, use fizzy ginger ale instead of champagne; nice, even if different. Also good poured over fruit salad.

Barbados grog

2 large oranges
20 cloves
1 litre red vin ordinaire
6 tablespoons rum
3 inch cinnamon stick
2 heaped tablespoons dark Barbados sugar

Stick the oranges with the cloves and put on a baking sheet in a hot oven for 20 minutes. Heat the wine, rum, cinnamon stick broken into pieces, and the sugar just to boiling point. Remove oranges from the oven, add to the wine mixture and simmer together for a few more minutes. Serve very hot.

Flaming punch

small bag mixed spices ($\frac{1}{2}$ oz)
1 litre red vin ordinaire
rind of 1 orange in thin strips
rind of 1 lemon in thin strips
4 oz sugar
5 fl oz brandy

Use whole pickling spices, tied in a muslin bag. Heat the wine with the bag of spices, fruit rinds and the sugar. Warm a large bowl and when the wine mixture is almost at boiling point pour it in, removing the bag of spices only. Have ready the brandy warmed in a small pan. Pour it in last and ignite at once. If you ladle the punch immediately into glasses the flame may last until all are served. This is served at Hallowe'en or any dark winter's night when it looks especially effective if the main lights are turned out and just a few candles kept alight.

Marlborough's mull

1 bottle full-bodied red wine
10 sugar lumps
4 cloves
15 fl oz boiling water
1 wineglass curaçao, or 1 wineglass brandy, or (after a battle) both

Bring the wine, sugar and cloves to the boil and add the boiling water. Stir well and add the curaçao and brandy (if desired). Pour into mugs or glasses over a silver spoon to prevent them from cracking. Serve very hot.
Note: The renowned Duke is said to have enjoyed this potion, which he generously shared with his wife, when at home, every night. Not all the battles referred to above took place overseas, as the Duchess was also a famous fighter.

Arancita calde

2 oranges
6 oz lump sugar
10 fl oz water
1 bottle full-bodied red wine
4 tablespoons brandy
orange slices to decorate

Rub the zest from the oranges with the sugar lumps then place them in a saucepan with the water and bring to the boil. Add the wine, brandy and juice from the oranges. Bring to the boil again and pour gently into small mugs or heatproof glasses and decorate each one with a slice of orange.

Rumfustian

1 tablespoon sugar
good pinch grated nutmeg
good pinch ground ginger
4 egg yolks
10 fl oz brown ale
1 bottle robust red wine
5 fl oz rum

Beat the sugar and spices into the egg yolks. Gradually add the beer, wine and rum over gentle heat, beating constantly. Do not allow the mixture to boil or stop beating as this might cause the egg yolks to curdle, but Rumfustian should be fairly thick. Serve it warm in punch glasses.

Le Brulot

5 fl oz plus 2 tablespoons rum
few drops vanilla essence
1 clove
pinch ground cinnamon
1 orange
2 oz sugar
15 fl oz china tea, freshly made and strained
2 tablespoons lemon juice

Put the 2 tablespoons of rum in a small basin with the vanilla essence, clove, cinnamon and finely grated zest from one quarter of the orange, and the juice from the whole orange. Allow to stand for an hour. Meanwhile, put the sugar in a heatproof punch bowl. Warm the rum in a small pan, ignite it and pour over the sugar. Strain the contents of the small basin into the punch bowl and add the tea and the lemon juice. Serve at once. (Serves 2.)

Krambambuli

1 tablespoon raisins
1 tablespoon chopped stoned dates
1 tablespoon chopped candied fruits
1 tablespoon chopped dried apricots
juice of 1 lemon
juice of 1 orange
8 oz lump sugar
10 fl oz dark rum
20 fl oz strong tea, strained
1 litre white wine

Place the fruit in a pan and pour over the fruit juice. Allow to stand until fruit is plump. Put the sugar in a metal sieve over the fruit, soak in rum and ignite. Heat together the tea and wine and pour into the pan after the rum has burnt out and sugar has dripped down into the fruit. Keep hot and strain into heated glasses.

Buttered rum

for each person:
3 tablespoons rum
small nut of butter
2 sugar lumps
pinch ground cinnamon or grated nutmeg
2 cloves
boiling water

Mix the ingredients together in a big mug, add boiling water to taste, stir and serve at once.

Stir a brimming tablespoon of Angostura Bitters into a glass of soda and gulp! Horrid, but may prevent or solace a hangover.

Lawn sleeves

1 large lemon
16 cloves
¼ teaspoon ground cinnamon
¼ teaspoon ground mace
¼ teaspoon ground allspice
¼ teaspoon ground ginger
10 fl oz water
1 bottle medium sweet sherry
4 oz sugar

Stick the lemon with the cloves and put it on a baking sheet in a hot oven (425°F, 220°C, Gas Mark 7) for 20 minutes. Place the spices in a saucepan with the water and boil until reduced by half. Heat the sherry separately with the lemon and sugar and add to the spiced water. Serve hot.

Note: Traditionally a small pot of calves' foot jelly is stirred into the mixture to make it more strengthening. This, to my mind, makes it rather nasty, but ½ oz powdered gelatine dissolved in a little hot water would not affect the flavour and is supposed to strengthen your fingernails!

'Serves eight genteel persons,' according to the original source, a housewife's hand-written recipe book dated 1873.

Gaelic coffee

for each person:
3 teaspoons caster sugar
1 tablespoon Scotch whisky, or Irish whiskey
5 fl oz hot strong coffee
4 tablespoons lightly whipped cream

If the coffee is lukewarm by the time it is served, it is spoiled. Rinse out the glasses with hot water to warm them beforehand, and dry thoroughly. Put the sugar in each glass, add the whisky and stir briskly. Pour the very hot strong black coffee over the sugar mixture and stir just until the sugar is dissolved. Have the cream ready, very lightly whipped, to pour in over the back of a spoon. Pour very gently and steadily so that the cream and coffee do not mix. Unwhipped cream can be used but requires more confidence and expertise. Don't forget whisky comes from Scotland, whiskey from Ireland. The Irish were first in the field with this superb combination of flavours, or so they say.

Café Napoléon: This excellent variation is made by using brandy instead of whisky.

Cooking with Wine

The wine you choose to drink ought always to be on friendly terms with the wine you have used in cooking. It may be a more aristocratic relation of a *vin ordinaire* or preferably a wine from the same region. For example, you may be fortunate enough to drink a Château bottled claret and cook with wine from a bottle labelled Médoc or simply Bordeaux – lesser wines but all grown in the same region of France. In some recipes, a robust or full-bodied red wine is recommended, otherwise light red wines are suitable. For savoury dishes generally, dry white wines are indicated, and a specific wine only if the dish is a regional one popular in the area where that particular wine is made.

How to use wine in cooking

When you add wine to a dish, remember that the cooking process is intended to evaporate or drive off the alcohol content almost entirely. All that should remain is the essential flavour of the wine itself.

Slow cooking: Wine which is added at the beginning of the long slow cooking of a casserole dish (or to a marinade in which the raw food is tenderized) will certainly become sufficiently mellow by the time the food is cooked. Wine used to roast joints considerably enhances the juices remaining in the pan which can be used both for basting and to make a rich sauce. If it is necessary to add wine towards the end of cooking a casserole, or if an extra rich flavour is required, reduce the wine by fast boiling it in a pan to one half or even one-third the original quantity. The alcohol will then have evaporated sufficiently, even if the reduced wine is added almost at the last moment.

Fast cooking: Where wine is added at the end of cooking, it must be boiled rapidly and reduced to a small quantity, otherwise the alcohol content will be too high and spoil the flavour. Such dishes are usually cooked in a wide shallow pan to aid rapid evaporation.

Interpreting recipes

Many recipes from other sources will simply state 'a wineglass' as a measure in the listed ingredients. Wine glasses may hold as little as 4 or as much as 8 fl oz of liquid so an average quantity to allow would be 5 to 6 fl oz, as the amount intended. In these recipes, quantities given will serve four people, and all spoon measures are level unless otherwise stated.

Hors d'oeuvre

A meal which begins well is likely to succeed right through to the coffee and liqueurs, just as a strong first act to a new play warms the critic's heart. Pamper your guests a little. Give them a change from the familiar melon wedge or grapefruit half coyly embedding a tired cherry. Sprinkle the cut grapefruit with brown sugar and rum and slip it under the grill until crisply golden; or slice your chilled melon into coupes of semi-sparkling white wine. When the seeds are removed from a halved Ogen or Charentais melon, the hollow that remains seems to invite a few spoonfuls of port. *Melon au porto* tastes as good as it looks, and may well be unfamiliar to your guests. An unusual first course, set ready on the table, enhances the welcoming effects of flowers and candlelight. Often it can be a conversation piece in itself.

Brandied grapefruit

2 grapefruit
4 oz demerara sugar
4 teaspoons brandy

Cut the grapefruit in half, loosen segments and remove membranes and pips. Cover each grapefruit half with sugar and sprinkle with brandy. Allow to stand for at least 30 minutes then place under a hot grill until the surface has melted and is bubbling. Serve very hot.

Three unusual starters with melon

Spiced melon cocktail

Cut the melon in half and remove the seeds. Scoop out the flesh with a melon baller. Dissolve 4 oz sugar in 5 fl oz water, flavour with a small cinnamon stick and 4 cloves. When the syrup is clear, remove spices. Add the melon balls and cook for a few minutes, until they became transparent. Drain. Add 4 tablespoons sweet white wine to the syrup and boil to reduce by one third. Pour over the melon balls, chill in the refrigerator, replace in the skins and serve cold.

Melon and grapefruit coupes

Prepare the melon as above, make the syrup but add a tablespoon of brandy instead of the white wine and reduce as before. Cut two grapefruit in half, spoon out the segments and add to the syrup with the melon balls. Chill and refill the mixture into the melon skins.

Tzigeuner melon

Prepare and scoop out melon flesh as for Spiced melon cocktail. Drain off the juice, toss the melon balls with a tablespoon each of diced lean ham, canned red pimiento, unpeeled cucumber and halved green and black olives. Moisten with wine vinaigrette sauce (see page 50) and pile into the melon skins.

Pears Roquefort

4 dessert pears
5 fl oz white wine
1 tablespoon lemon juice
2 oz blue cheese (Roquefort or Danish Blue)
2 tablespoons soured cream
salt and freshly ground white pepper
paprika

Peel, halve and core the pears straight into a dish containing the wine and lemon juice. Mash the cheese, work in the cream and lastly drain the pears and beat enough of the wine left in the dish into the mixture to make it creamy. Stuff the pear halves

with this, seasoning lightly to taste. Dust lightly with paprika and serve at once before the pears discolour.

Far eastern fruit coupes

1 small fresh pineapple
2 oz drained lychees
2 oz drained maraschino cherries
1–2 tablespoons icing sugar, sieved
2–3 tablespoons brandy

Peel and slice the pineapple, remove hard core and dice the flesh. Place the pineapple pieces in a dish and add the lychees and cherries. Add sugar and brandy. Stir gently then chill for at least 2 hours before serving in individual glass dishes.

Crevettes au cari

$\frac{1}{2}$ oz butter
8 oz potted shrimps
8 oz button mushrooms
1 teaspoon lemon juice
$\frac{1}{2}$ teaspoon curry powder
2 tablespoons medium dry sherry
4 slices white bread
1 tablespoon chopped parsley to garnish

Melt the butter in a small saucepan and then add the potted shrimps. Warm through until butter is melted, then add the thinly sliced mushrooms. Cook gently for about 4 minutes then add the lemon juice, curry powder and sherry and bring to boiling point, stirring constantly.

Meanwhile, toast the bread, trim off crusts and place on a hot serving dish. Divide the shrimp and mushroom mixture between the hot toast slices and sprinkle with parsley before serving.

Anchoiade

2 2-oz cans anchovy fillets
2 cloves garlic, crushed
1 tablespoon brandy
1 oz butter
1–2 tablespoons olive oil
freshly ground black pepper

Nothing works better than a pestle and mortar, but a blender could be used. Pound the anchovy fillets, oil from the can, crushed garlic, brandy and butter together to make a smooth paste, adding extra olive oil a few drops at a time, and seasoning with pepper at the end. Serve as an appetiser on hot toast.

Cozze alla Veronelli

3 pints mussels
8 fl oz dry white wine
2 teaspoons powdered gelatine
2 oz can anchovy fillets, drained
2 oz butter
parsley sprigs to garnish

Cook the mussels in the wine as for Cozze capricciose (see opposite) but reduce the liquor to 6 fl oz. Dissolve the gelatine in 2 tablespoons hot water, stir into the liquor and chill until the mixture becomes syrupy. Meanwhile, pound the anchovy fillets with the butter until smooth. Take half the mussel shells, choosing the better shaped ones, and spoon a little anchovy butter into each. Place a chilled mussel on top, coat with the partially set aspic, then mask them completely. Chill and when firmly set serve garnished with parsley sprigs.

Cozze capricciose

2 pints mussels
5 fl oz dry white wine
5 fl oz mayonnaise
1 tablespoon mild continental mustard
8 oz tiny new boiled potatoes
2 tablespoons cooked peas
2 tablespoons chopped parsley to garnish

Scrub the mussels and remove the beards. Place in a heavy pan with the wine, cover tightly and shake occasionally over a high heat for a few minutes, or until all the shells are open. Drain the mussels through a colander, reserving the liquor, cool and remove them from their shells. Boil the liquor hard until reduced to 4 tablespoons. Strain again through a fine sieve. Chill the mussels and the liquid separately. Combine the liquid, mayonnaise and mustard, then fold in the mussels, potatoes and peas and serve sprinkled with chopped parsley.

Eingelegte Heringe

1 large onion
6 fresh herrings
2 tablespoons double cream
salt and freshly ground black pepper
1 tablespoon pickling spice
10 fl oz dry white wine
5 fl oz soured cream

Slice the onion finely. Take one slice and chop it finely. Split the herrings and remove the bones. Spread the fillets with finely chopped onion, double cream, and seasoning and roll them up. Put half the onion slices in the bottom of a shallow ovenproof dish, place the 12 herring rolls

Halibut in White Wine Sauce

on this and sprinkle over the pickling spice and seasoning. Pour over the wine then cover with the remaining onion and more seasoning. Cover lightly with foil and cook in a moderate oven (350°F, 180°C, Gas Mark 4) for 15 minutes. Remove fish to a serving dish. Strain the liquor from the baking dish, add the soured cream and mix well. Pour over the fish and serve cold as an hors d'oeuvre for 6.

Pâté de Cassis

8 oz lean pork
8 oz fat pork
8 oz pigs' liver
1 onion
8 oz veal
2 oz soft white breadcrumbs
4 fl oz red wine
1 teaspoon dried marjoram
pinch ground allspice
salt and freshly ground black pepper
2 eggs, beaten
3 bay leaves
6 juniper berries

Mince the three pork meats and the onion together twice and place in a bowl. Dice the veal finely and mix in. Sprinkle over the breadcrumbs and pour over the wine. Leave to stand for 10 minutes, then mix well. Add herbs, allspice, seasonings and beaten eggs. Pack the mixture firmly into a shallow ovenproof earthenware dish and smooth the top. Arrange the bay leaves and juniper berries over the mixture and cover the dish with foil. Place in a *bain marie* and cook in a moderate oven (350°F, 180°C, Gas Mark 4) for about 1½ hours, until firm. Allow to cool and mature for at least 24 hours before serving from the dish.

Chicken liver terrine 'en suprise'

2 tablespoons port
5 fl oz dry white wine
pinch grated nutmeg or mace
1½ lbs chicken livers
1 oz butter
1 white bread roll soaked in water
8 oz pork sausagemeat
salt and freshly ground white pepper
6 thin rashers streaky bacon

Make a marinade with the port, wine and spice, and place the chicken livers in this for several hours. Drain. Melt the butter and use to cook the livers lightly until just firm but very pink in the centre. Reserve 4 of the livers whole. Mince the remaining livers, or use a blender. Squeeze out the bread roll. Blend the minced livers with the sausagemeat, bread and seasoning. Remove rinds from bacon and stretch well with a knife. If not thin enough bat out between layers of paper as for veal escalopes. Use bacon to line a terrine or small loaf tin, across the bottom and up the sides. Put half the chicken liver mixture in the bottom, arrange the 4 whole livers on this, and cover with the remaining mixture. Cover mould with foil, place in a *bain marie* and cook in a moderate oven (350°F, 180°C, Gas Mark 4) for 1 to 1¼ hours. Remove and cool. Chill in the refrigerator and allow to mature at least 2 days before turning out and serving.

Stuffed olives, excellent in cooked dishes, will also freeze (leave plenty of headspace); a few chopped up, add zest to these pâtés.

Spanish Chicken with Olives

Mushrooms à la Grecque

1 small onion
4 tablespoons olive oil
1 lb button mushrooms
1 tablespoon tomato purée
4 tablespoons white wine
3 tablespoons lemon juice
1 bay leaf
½ teaspoon ground coriander
salt and freshly ground black pepper

Chop the onion finely. Heat the oil in a frying pan and use to cook the onion gently until limp. Add the mushrooms and sauté until they are coated with oil all over. Mix together the tomato purée, wine and lemon juice and add to the pan with the bay leaf and seasonings. Cover and simmer gently for 8 minutes, or until the mushrooms are just tender. Discard bay leaf. Remove the mushrooms with a slotted draining spoon and boil the liquid hard to reduce by one third. Pour the reduced liquid over the mushrooms and chill.

Mushrooms à l'instant

8 oz button mushrooms
2 oz butter
2 tablespoons dry sherry
salt and freshly ground white pepper
4 fl oz sour cream

Remove mushroom stalks and start these cooking in the butter while you slice up the caps. Stir in, cooking until the juice starts to run, then add the sherry and season lightly to taste. When mushrooms are barely golden, remove from heat and stir in the cream. Serve at once, hot, with fingers of toast.

Courgettes à la Chantal

1½ oz butter
2 tablespoons chopped onion
1 tablespoon grated carrot
1 clove garlic, crushed
2 oz mushrooms, sliced
5 fl oz dry white wine
5 fl oz water
1 bouquet garni
1 lb small courgettes
salt and freshly ground black pepper

Melt the butter and fry the onion, carrot and garlic in it over gentle heat, stirring until softened. Add the mushrooms and cook for another minute. Add the wine, water and *bouquet garni*. Bring to the boil, cover and simmer for 15 minutes. Do not peel the courgettes completely but remove strips of the peel with a decorative *'cannel'* knife, or peel in stripes. Slice thinly. Add to the pan, season, cover and simmer until courgettes are just tender but not mushy. Remove bouquet garni and transfer to a serving dish. Serve chilled.

Oignons Grand Veneur

5 fl oz dry white wine
4 tablespoons wine vinegar
2 oz brown sugar
2 oz seedless raisins
2 tablespoons tomato purée
2 tablespoons olive oil
salt and freshly ground black pepper
1 lb small pickling onions
1 tablespoon chopped chervil or parsley to garnish

Place the first six ingredients in a pan and season lightly with salt and pepper. Bring to the boil, cover and simmer for 20

Italian Lamb Stew

minutes. Add the onions and continue cooking until they are just tender. Adjust seasoning if necessary, chill and serve cold sprinkled with chopped chervil if available, or with chopped parsley.

Salade Côte d'Azur

1 small lettuce
4 canned or frozen artichoke hearts
7 oz can tuna fish
12 black olives
2 sticks celery, chopped
1 tablespoon flaked almonds
wine vinaigrette dressing:
½ teaspoon salt
¼ teaspoon freshly ground black pepper
½ teaspoon French mustard
1 tablespoon wine vinegar
3 tablespoons dry white wine
4 tablespoons olive oil

Wash the lettuce well and tear into small pieces. Divide between 4 individual salad bowls. Place an artichoke heart in the centre of each bowl. Surround with piles of drained and flaked tuna, olives, celery and almonds. Whisk together all the ingredients for the dressing, adding the olive oil last, a few drops at a time. Pour over the salads and serve immediately.

Spicy yoghourt dressing

4 teaspoons olive oil
1 teaspoon lemon juice
2 tablespoons white wine
salt and freshly ground black pepper
5 oz carton natural yoghourt
½ teaspoon Worcestershire sauce
1 tablespoon finely chopped parsley

Beat together the oil, lemon juice, wine and seasoning and leave to stand for 30 minutes. Gradually beat in the yoghourt with the Worcestershire sauce and parsley. Taste and adjust seasoning. Serve with salads such as celery, onion, cooked potato, sautéed mushrooms.

Note: The basic dressing for a green salad can be varied. Add very finely chopped shallots or chives or the green part of spring onions. Chopped capers, or any delicately flavoured fresh herbs such as parsley and mint, can also be included. It can also be used as a basis for other salads.

Italian salad

4 tablespoons white wine
5 fl oz olive oil
2 teaspoons capers, drained
salt and freshly ground black pepper
8 oz button mushrooms, sliced
1 small cucumber
1 green pepper
2 oz can anchovy fillets
1 hard boiled egg yolk
2 tomatoes, quartered, to garnish

Make a marinade with the wine, olive oil, capers and seasoning. Add the mushrooms and leave to marinade for an hour. Peel and dice the cucumber and deseed and slice the pepper. Add these to the marinade and toss lightly together. Pound the anchovy fillets with their oil then beat in the egg yolk. Spread this dressing over the salad and garnish with the tomato quarters.

Fresh fruit cocktail with vinaigrette dressing

Different kinds of melon, with their delicate colour contrasts and difference in flavour, make an exciting blend dressed with a slightly sweetened wine vinaigrette. Include peeled black or white grapes, split almonds or roughly chopped walnuts for a different texture.

Raw mushroom and cauliflower salad

8 oz button mushrooms, sliced
8 oz blanched cauliflower florets
6 tablespoons wine vinaigrette dressing (see page 50)
salt and freshly ground black pepper
1 tablespoon chopped parsley, to garnish

The cauliflower can be used raw, or just blanched in fast boiling salted water for a minute. Combine the mushroom and cauliflower, pour the dressing over and add extra seasoning. Toss together very lightly and chill for at least 2 hours. Serve sprinkled with the parsley.

Red jewel salad

1 raspberry jelly tablet
8 fl oz boiling water
4 fl oz dry red wine
1 tablespoon lemon juice
1-lb jar or can whole cranberry sauce
1 teaspoon grated orange zest

Break up the jelly tablet, add to the boiling water and stir until melted. Gradually add the wine and lemon juice, stir, then set aside until cool and just beginning to set. Add cranberry sauce and orange zest, stir well and pour into a rinsed mould, or into individual moulds. Chill until set. Unmould and serve with roast turkey or chicken.

Paprika cream dressing

3 eggs
2 oz caster sugar
salt
1 teaspoon paprika pepper
5 fl oz canned pineapple juice
5 fl oz white wine

Whisk the eggs with the sugar, a pinch of salt and the paprika in a double boiler over simmering water until foamy. Whisk in the pineapple juice and wine, and continue whisking until thick and spongy in texture. Cool, pour into a sauceboat and chill. Serve with salads including both fruit and green salad vegetables.

Pickled herring salad

4 pickled herring fillets, drained
6 tablespoons wine vinaigrette dressing (see page 50)
2 tablespoons cream
2 green skinned dessert apples
1 large or 2 small cooked potatoes, diced
1 dill pickle, chopped
6 spring onions, chopped, to garnish

Dice the herrings and marinade them in the dressing for at least an hour. Lightly whip the cream and stir in. Core and dice the apples without peeling them. Fold the apple, potato and dill pickle into the herring mixture. Serve sprinkled with the chopped spring onion.

Soups, sauces and marinades

Today, when a home made soup is something rare, it is flattering to be offered one which your hostess has made herself. Soups made with wine come in great variety: delicate fish soups, hearty 'gamey' ones, even sweet fruit soups. Polish cherry soup, for instance, is a surprise to western European palates, but makes a refreshing introduction to any meal. As for sauces, they encompass the whole world of wine. My Cranberry sauce is a newcomer among the classics like Madeira Sauce or Bourguignon but try it. Red wine syrup has a natural appeal for sweet lovers who have no rum or liqueur in the house. Last come marinades which do so much to enhance and tenderize all sorts of meat.

Polish cherry soup

5 fl oz red wine
2 strips orange rind
¼ teaspoon ground cinnamon
pinch ground cloves
½ oz cornflour
15 fl oz water
15 oz can Morello cherries, stoned
1 tablespoon sugar if required
4 tablespoons soured cream to garnish

Simmer the wine with the fruit rind and spices over gentle heat for 5 minutes, then remove rind. Moisten the cornflour with a little water, add remaining water to the wine with the cherries and syrup from the can. Heat and then stir in the moistened cornflour and bring to the boil, stirring constantly. Cook for 2 minutes. Taste and add a little sugar if desired. Allow to cool, stirring occasionally to prevent a skin forming. Chill and serve in soup coupes each garnished with soured cream.

Plum soup

1 orange
2 lbs red plums
8 oz raisins
30 fl oz water
4 oz sugar
12 cloves
scant ½ oz gelatine
5 fl oz Cinzano Bianco
5 fl oz double or soured cream

Finely grate the zest from the orange. Place the orange in a saucepan and crush roughly with a wooden spoon. Stone the plums and add pulp to orange with the raisins, water, sugar and cloves. Bring to the boil and cook for 15 minutes. Strain and dissolve gelatine in the hot soup. Stir in the wine, cool and chill in the refrigerator for at least 3 hours. Serve from a tureen and garnish each serving with a swirl of cream and a sprinkling of orange zest.

Russian melon soup

1 lb melon flesh
4 oz peeled cucumber
8 fl oz dry white wine
3 oz sugar
5 fl oz water
1 tablespoon lemon juice
5 fl oz sour cream

Chop the melon and cucumber roughly and liquidize in the blender with the wine. Dissolve the sugar in the water, bring to the boil and simmer for 4 minutes. Cool. Add syrup to the melon and cucumber purée according to the sweetness of the melon. Finally stir in the lemon juice and sour cream. Serve chilled.

Spring blossom soup

1 chicken stock cube
4 spring onions, trimmed
½ cucumber, unpeeled
5 fl oz dry white wine
½ teaspoon dried dill weed
1 tablespoon chopped parsley
salt and freshly ground white pepper
5 fl oz single cream

Dissolve the stock cube in a few table-spoons of boiling water then add 10 fl oz cold water. Cut some spring onion rings and reserve for the garnish. Liquidize the remaining spring onions, the cucumber and chicken stock in the blender. Stir in the wine, herbs and seasoning. Add most of the cream and stir until well blended. Serve in chilled soup coupes, garnished with a spiral of cream and onion rings.

Bohnensuppe

8 oz red kidney beans
60 fl oz water
salt and freshly ground black pepper
1 large onion, sliced
1 large carrot, sliced
½ teaspoon dried thyme
1 bay leaf
6 fl oz red wine
2 oz butter

Soak the beans overnight in cold water. Drain and place in a saucepan with the measured water and salt. Bring to the boil, add the onion, carrot, herbs and wine. Return to the boil, cover and simmer gently until the beans are tender. Remove bay leaf and sieve or liquidize the soup. Adjust seasoning, bring to the boil again, stir in the butter. (Serves 8.)

Two-cucumber soup

½ cucumber, peeled
1 small dill-pickled cucumber, chopped
3 spring onions, chopped
4 oz cooked new potatoes, diced
4 oz cooked ham, diced
5 fl oz soured cream
1 teaspoon German mustard
1 teaspoon sugar
10 fl oz dry white wine
20 fl oz chicken stock
½ teaspoon dried dill
salt and freshly ground black pepper
chopped chervil and parsley

Dice the fresh peeled cucumber evenly and place in a large bowl with the pickled cucumber, onions, potatoes and ham. Mix together the cream, mustard, sugar and wine and pour over the mixture. Next pour over the chicken stock and stir well. Add the dill, taste and add seasoning to taste. Chopped fresh chervil and parsley can be added if available. Chill. Stir the soup as you serve it otherwise the vegetables stay at the bottom.

Rote Rübensuppe

1 small cooked beetroot
1 tablespoon tomato purée
15 oz can consommé
4 tablespoons dry sherry
salt and freshly ground black pepper
4 tablespoons cream

Chop the beetroot roughly and liquidize in the blender with the tomato purée and consommé. Place in a saucepan and when nearly boiling add the sherry and adjust seasoning. Stir the cream lightly through the soup as you pour into the soup bowls, to give a marbled effect.

Dicke Zwiebelsuppe

12 oz onions
1½ oz butter
2 tablespoons cornflour
30 fl oz chicken stock
5 fl oz dry white wine
4 tablespoons cream
salt and freshly ground white pepper
finely grated nutmeg
1 tablespoon finely chopped watercress to garnish

Chop the onions very finely. Melt the butter and use to cook the onions gently until transparent but not coloured. Add the cornflour and stir until smooth. Gradually add the stock and wine and bring to the boil, stirring constantly. Cover and simmer for 30 minutes. Remove from the heat, stir in the cream and adjust seasoning. Pour into individual soup coupes and garnish each with a little finely chopped watercress.

Bisque de coquilles

2 tablespoons oil
1 carrot, chopped
1 large mild onion, chopped
4 oz white fish fillets, diced
4 tablespoons flour
5 fl oz water
2 tablespoons tomato purée
5 fl oz white wine
25 fl oz milk
6 scallops
salt and freshly ground white pepper
3 tablespoons double cream

Heat the oil and use to fry the carrot and onion until softened but not browned.

Add the white fish and fry for a further 5 minutes. Stir in the flour until well blended then gradually add the water, tomato purée, and wine. Bring to the boil, stirring constantly. Add the milk, bring back to the boil, cover and simmer gently for 30 minutes. Liquidize or sieve and place in a clean saucepan. Dice the scallops, add to the soup and bring to the boil. Cook for 10 minutes. Adjust seasoning, stir in the cream and reheat but do not allow to boil.

Saffron fish soup

2 lbs mixed fish (small mackerel, lemon sole, fresh haddock, shelled cooked prawns or shrimps)
6 tablespoons olive oil
1 leek, chopped
1 onion, chopped
3 cloves garlic, crushed
good pinch powdered saffron
½ teaspoon dried fennel
salt and freshly ground black pepper
5 fl oz dry white wine
25 fl oz water
3 strips orange rind
1 egg yolk

Have the fish cleaned, boned and roughly chopped; leave the shellfish whole. Reserve fish trimmings. Heat 4 tablespoons of the oil and use to fry the leek, onion and garlic until soft and golden. Add the fish trimmings, bring to the boil and skim if necessary. Add the spices, herbs, seasonings, wine, water and orange rind. Return to the boil, cover and simmer for 15 minutes. Strain the stock into a clean pan, add the chopped raw fish and bring to the boil. Cover and simmer for 10 minutes, then add the shellfish and cook for a further 2 or 3 minutes. Put egg yolk in a soup tureen and beat in the remaining oil, a little at a time, to make a mayonnaise. Gradually stir in the boiling soup. Serve with slices of French bread spread with crushed garlic and grated gruyère cheese, then toasted.

Mussel soup

1 oz butter
½ oz flour
1 quart mussels
6 fl oz dry white wine
2 egg yolks
4 tablespoons double cream
1 tablespoon chopped parsley
fish stock:
1 lb sole bones
1 onion, sliced
4 white peppercorns
1 oz butter
bouquet garni
2 tablespoons lemon juice
salt
1 clove garlic, crushed
6 fl oz dry white wine
25 fl oz water

To make the fish stock, put the rinsed fish bones in a saucepan with the other ingredients, bring to the boil, cover and simmer for 30 minutes. Melt 1 oz butter in a large saucepan, stir in the flour and cook gently until golden. Strain in the fish stock and bring to the boil, stirring constantly. Cover and simmer for 15 minutes. Scrub the mussels and put them in a saucepan with the remaining wine. Bring to the boil and simmer for a minute. Strain the liquor into the soup. Shell the mussels, discarding any that have not opened, and add them to the soup.

Simmer for 5 minutes. Mix together the egg yolks and cream, stir in a little of the hot soup, then add this mixture to the soup and reheat without boiling. Stir in the parsley just before serving.

Rich kidney soup

8 oz ox kidney
40 fl oz beef stock
bouquet garni
1 oz butter
1 onion, chopped
2 tablespoons flour
1 tablespoon tomato purée
6 fl oz dry red wine
salt and freshly ground black pepper

Wash, skin, cut in half and core the kidney then rinse in cold water and place in a pan with half the stock and the bouquet garni. Bring to the boil, cover and simmer for an hour, until the kidney is very tender. Discard bouquet garni. Melt the butter in a large saucepan, and use to cook the onion gently until browned. Stir in the flour and tomato purée until well blended. Gradually add the remaining stock and bring to the boil, stirring constantly. Stir in the wine, cooked kidney and stock, taste and adjust seasoning. Bring back to boiling point, cover and simmer for 15 minutes. Liquidize or sieve and serve fried bread croûtons separately.

Strain any leftover rich wine soup, add dry sherry to white wine, port to red wine soup, thicken, serve with grilled fish or meat.

Game soup

carcass of 1 cooked pheasant and 2 partridges;
   or 1 old pheasant
4 beef stock cubes
70 fl oz boiling water
1 large onion, sliced
1 turnip, chopped
4 carrots, chopped
2 sticks celery, chopped
2 rashers bacon, chopped
10 fl oz red wine
2 tablespoons tomato purée
1 clove
9 peppercorns
salt

Place the game bones, or pheasant in a large saucepan. Make up the stock cubes with the boiling water and add to the saucepan with the remaining ingredients. Bring to the boil, cover and simmer gently for about 3 hours. Adjust seasoning and strain. (Serves 8.)

Note: The old country method is to use bones, and to bake them first in the oven until brown to give a rich colour.

The Squire's hare soup

4 oz butter
8 oz lean bacon
hare giblets and any uncooked trimmings
2 onions, chopped
4 shallots, chopped
12 peppercorns
$\frac{1}{4}$ teaspoon ground mace
bouquet garni
80 fl oz stock
5 fl oz red wine
2 oz flour
4 tablespoons port

Heat half the butter and use to fry the bacon and hare pieces for 5 minutes. Add the onions, shallots, peppercorns, mace, bouquet garni, stock and wine. Bring to the boil, cover and simmer for about 3 hours. Skim and strain the stock. Melt the remaining butter in a clean pan, stir in the flour and cook gently until pale golden. Gradually stir in the strained stock and bring to the boil, stirring constantly. Add the port and simmer for a further 20 minutes. Adjust seasoning. Dice any of the meat remaining from the cooked hare and add to the soup. (Serves 8.)

Shrewsbury sauce

2 beef stock cubes
20 fl oz boiling water
1 oz butter
$1\frac{1}{2}$ oz flour
10 fl oz full-bodied red wine
2 teaspoons tomato purée
$\frac{1}{4}$ teaspoon dried mixed herbs
3 tablespoons redcurrant jelly
little extra butter

Dissolve the stock cubes in the boiling water. Melt the butter in a saucepan and stir in the flour. Cook for 1 minute. Gradually add the stock and wine and bring to the boil, stirring constantly. Add the tomato purée and herbs, cover and simmer gently for at least an hour. Skim if necessary and stir from time to time. The sauce should be only thick enough to coat the back of a spoon. To serve, add the jelly and reheat very slowly, stirring, to melt the jelly. A dot or two more butter added before serving gives the sauce an extra gloss.

My herbed mushroom sauce

1 oz butter
4 oz button mushrooms, sliced
2 oz chopped onion
4 fl oz dry white wine
2 tablespoons tomato purée
herbs to taste

Melt the butter and use to sauté the mushrooms and onion until pale golden. Add the wine, tomato purée and 1 tablespoon fresh chopped herbs (parsley, marjoram, thyme, basil, oregano, winter savory) or 1 tablespoon dried herbs. Bring to the boil and simmer for 5 minutes. The more strongly flavoured herbs will predominate over the mushrooms, but the sauce can be adapted to suit most fish or white meat dishes.

Sauce matelote

20 fl oz full-bodied red wine
3 oz butter
1 small onion, chopped
2 oz flour
½ teaspoon sugar
salt and freshly ground black pepper

Heat the wine until nearly boiling. In another pan, melt the butter and use to cook the onion gently until golden. Sprinkle in the flour and stir over moderate heat until well blended. Add the wine and cook, stirring constantly, until slightly thickened. If possible, caramelise the sugar in an old spoon over a flame and stir into the sauce or, as a substitute, add a few drops of gravy browning and rather less sugar.

Sauce Bourguignonne

1 small onion
1 tablespoon chopped parsley
¼ teaspoon dried thyme
1 small bay leaf
15 fl oz full-bodied red wine, preferably Burgundy
2 oz mushrooms
1 oz butter
¾ oz flour
salt and freshly ground black pepper

Chop the onion finely and place in a saucepan with the herbs, bay leaf and wine. Chop the mushrooms, add to the pan and stir well. Bring to the boil and simmer uncovered until reduced by half. Strain carefully into a clean saucepan. Knead together the butter and flour and add to the sauce in small pieces. Stir briskly until sauce is smooth and thickened. Cook for 2 minutes and season to taste.

Cranberry sauce

3 oz sugar
4 tablespoons water
8 oz cranberries
2 oz raisins
¼ teaspoon ground cinnamon
4 tablespoons port

Dissolve the sugar in the water over gentle heat. Add the cranberries, raisins and cinnamon and cook until tender. Add the port, cook for one further minute. Cool slightly, sieve or liquidize. Serve with chicken, turkey or game.

Devilling sauce

4 tablespoons oil
2 large onions, grated
5 fl oz full-bodied red wine
1 tablespoon Worcestershire sauce
1 teaspoon Tabasco
$\frac{1}{4}$ teaspoon curry powder
$\frac{1}{4}$ teaspoon salt

Heat the oil and use to fry the grated onion until softened but not coloured. Stir in all the other ingredients and bring to the boil, stirring constantly. Use to brush meat or poultry for grilling just before cooking and baste with the sauce several times during cooking. The remaining liquid can be strained, added to an equal quantity of stock and slightly thickened with cornflour to make a devilled sauce to serve with the dish.

Madeira sauce

3 oz butter
2 oz flour
6 fl oz hot strong beef stock
4 fl oz Madeira
salt and freshly ground black pepper

Melt the butter in a small pan, allow to brown slightly, then stir in the flour and cook, stirring, for a few moments without allowing to become dark brown. Add the hot stock a little at a time, beating it in over moderate heat until the sauce is thick and smooth. Add the Madeira, still beating, season to taste and barely simmer for a further 2–3 minutes.

Note: the secret is to brown the butter before adding the flour, and not to cook long after adding the Madeira.

Salsa al vino bianco

8 fl oz dry white wine
1 small onion, sliced
3 egg yolks
1 teaspoon lemon juice
4–6 oz butter

Bring the wine to the boil, add the sliced onion and boil down until liquid is reduced to one quarter (2 fl oz). Strain and allow to stand until cool. Put the egg yolks in a double boiler, add the wine and lemon juice and beat over simmering water until well blended. Add the butter, a little at a time, until thickened. Beat constantly, and do not allow the sauce to boil.

Note: This is an Italian version of Hollandaise sauce, requiring not so much butter, and is very good over most vegetables and with fish.

Bigarrade sauce

2 oranges
5 fl oz giblet stock
$\frac{1}{2}$ oz cornflour
2 teaspoons brown sugar
2 tablespoons sweet sherry or port

Grate the zest from the oranges and squeeze the juice. Bring the zest to the boil in the stock and simmer for 7–8 minutes. Blend the cornflour with a little cold water, strain in the stock, stir well and return to the pan. Add the sugar and cook gently until sauce is smooth and thick. Add the sherry and simmer for a further 2 minutes. Serve with duck, goose, etc.

Sour cherry sauce

15 oz can morello cherries, stoned
1 tablespoon cornflour
4 fl oz dry red wine
pinch salt
1 strip lemon rind
pinch cinnamon

Use a little cherry syrup to moisten the cornflour, put all remaining ingredients into a small saucepan. Bring to the boil, add the moistened cornflour and stir constantly until thickened. Cook for 5 minutes. Serve with hot ham or tongue.

Apricot sherry sauce

3 tablespoons sugar
4 fl oz water
4 fl oz dry sherry
4 tablespoons apricot jam
few drops lemon juice

Place the sugar and water in a saucepan, bring to the boil and simmer for 8 minutes. Add the sherry and apricot jam and return to the boil, stirring constantly. Add a little lemon juice then strain into a sauce boat.

Rich rum syrup

6 tablespoons sugar
4 tablespoons rum
2 tablespoons lemon juice
1 teaspoon finely grated lemon zest

Place all the ingredients in a small saucepan and heat until the sugar has completely dissolved. This is much more concentrated than the rum-flavoured syrup used to soak a savarin cake, and is more suitable to serve over vanilla or almond flavoured puddings.

Wein sauce

10 fl oz red wine
10 fl oz red fruit juice or orange juice
3 oz sugar
$\frac{1}{4}$ teaspoon cinnamon
1 clove
$\frac{1}{2}$ oz cornflour

Place the wine in a saucepan with the fruit juice, sugar, cinnamon and clove. Bring to boiling point. Moisten the cornflour with a little cold water, add to the pan and bring to the boil again, stirring constantly until sauce is thickened and clear. Serve hot or cold.

Caribbean sauce

2 ripe bananas
4 oz caster sugar
2 tablespoons Curaçao or Cointreau
10 fl oz double cream

Peel the bananas and rub them through a sieve. Place in a small saucepan with the sugar and liqueur. Heat, stirring, until the sugar has dissolved and bring to boiling point. Remove from the heat and chill. Whip the cream and fold into the cold banana mixture.

Chaudeau

10 fl oz white wine
1 tablespoon lemon juice
$2\frac{1}{2}$ oz sugar
2 eggs
1 teaspoon cornflour
1 teaspoon finely grated lemon zest

Place all the ingredients in a double boiler over gently boiling water and beat continuously until doubled in volume.

Red wine marinade – cooked

2 tablespoons olive oil
1 medium onion, sliced
1 carrot, sliced
1 stick celery, sliced
4 fl oz full-bodied red wine
2 tablespoons wine vinegar
30 fl oz water
3 bay leaves
6 juniper berries
1 teaspoon sugar
1 tablespoon salt
12 peppercorns

Heat the oil and use to sauté the onion, carrot and celery gently for 2 minutes. Add the remaining ingredients and bring to the boil. Cover and simmer gently until the vegetables are soft, about 25 minutes. Remove from heat and pour hot marinade over the meat. Allow to stand for 2 to 3 days. Each day, strain off the liquid, bring to the boil and pour again over the meat. Suitable for game.

Strong marinade

20 fl oz full-bodied red wine
4 fl oz wine vinegar
2 carrots, sliced
2 oz onion, minced
3 cloves
$\frac{1}{4}$ teaspoon freshly ground black pepper
$\frac{1}{2}$ teaspoon dried thyme
1 bay leaf
1 clove garlic, crushed

Place all ingredients in a saucepan and bring to the boil. Simmer for 5 minutes. Cool, pour over the meat and allow to stand overnight. Suitable for strongly flavoured meats.

Red wine marinade – uncooked

20 fl oz red wine
5 fl oz malt vinegar
2 tablespoons oil
1 carrot, sliced
2 onions, chopped
8 peppercorns
3 cloves
sprig rosemary
$\frac{1}{4}$ teaspoon dried thyme
sprig parsley
2 bay leaves

Mix all the ingredients together. Allow to stand for 24 hours. Marinate joints for 24 to 48 hours in this, small cuts overnight only. Suitable for lean game and red meat.

Honey marinade

5 fl oz sweet red wine
4 tablespoons white vinegar
4 tablespoons clear honey
pinch ground cinnamon
pinch ground mace

Mix together all the ingredients, pour over the meat and leave for 2 to 3 hours. Use to baste the meat during cooking. Suitable for poultry, pork or ham.

Sherry marinade

5 fl oz orange or pineapple juice
2 tablespoons sweet sherry
1 tablespoon oil
1 tablespoon tomato ketchup
2 teaspoons mild continental mustard
$\frac{1}{2}$ teaspoon ground ginger
$\frac{1}{2}$ teaspoon salt

Combine all the ingredients in a saucepan and bring very slowly to the boil, stirring.

Honey Marinade

Simmer for 5 minutes and when cool, use as a basting sauce. Suitable for pork and ham.

White wine marinade – cooked

10 fl oz dry white wine
2 tablespoons olive oil
few drops Tabasco sauce
3 large strips orange rind
2 sprigs mint
½ teaspoon dried oregano
salt and freshly ground white pepper

Place all the ingredients in a saucepan and bring to the boil. Allow to cool and stand overnight. Strain over the meat and leave for 2 to 3 hours. Suitable for poultry and veal.

Rosé wine marinade

5 fl oz tarragon vinegar
5 fl oz water
1 small carrot, diced
2 sticks celery, chopped
1 large onion, chopped
1 teaspoon chopped green ginger
1 teaspoon ground coriander
1 sprig parsley
10 fl oz rosé wine

Place all ingredients, with the exception of the wine, in a saucepan and bring to the boil. Add the wine and bring to the boil again. Cool slightly, pour over the meat while still warm. Allow to stand for 12 to 24 hours. Suitable for poultry and white meat.

Fish and shellfish

Fresh, crisp white wines from the region of the Loire or the Rhine seem made to drink with fish. The combination is so perfect. You may find one or two surprises in this section since I am especially fond of fish cooked with a delicate vin rosé and of course will drink a rosé with it. Trout and other oily fish seem to develop a special flavour when cooked in rosé though I have never quite come to enjoy the flavour of sole in red wine! It does not 'speak' to me as the French say, and it is not given here.

Scampi shells

8 oz white fish fillets
8 oz uncooked shelled scampi
5 fl oz dry white wine
15 oz can cream of scampi soup
1 lb mashed potatoes
3 oz butter
1 egg
¼ teaspoon grated nutmeg
little milk
parsley sprigs to garnish

Poach the fish and scampi in the wine until tender, then drain and flake the fish. Boil the fish liquor hard until reduced to 2 tablespoons and stir in the soup. Continue boiling, stirring constantly, until reduced by one third. Divide the fish mixture between 4 deep scallop shells and spoon over the soup. Beat potato until smooth with 2 oz butter, the lightly beaten egg and nutmeg. Add sufficient milk to give a smooth piping consistency. Pipe a border of potato round the edge of the shells. Melt the remaining butter and spoon over the shells then bake in a hot oven (425°F, 220°C, Gas Mark 7) for 20 minutes. Garnish with sprigs of parsley.

Stewed oysters

24 small oysters
1 bay leaf
2 oz butter
few drops Tabasco sauce
salt and freshly ground black pepper
good pinch paprika pepper
10 fl oz warm milk
4 tablespoons dry sherry
4 tablespoons cream
pinch grated nutmeg

Put the oysters and their liquor in a pan with the bay leaf, butter, tabasco, salt, pepper and paprika. Bring to the boil, cover and simmer until the edges of the oysters get frilly. Remove the bay leaf, add the warm milk and stir gently to reheat. Add the sherry, bring just to simmering point and stir in the cream. Adjust seasoning if necessary. Serve in small bowls, dusted with nutmeg.

Court bouillon

20 fl water
10 fl oz wine
1 onion, sliced
1 carrot, sliced
bouquet garni
1 teaspoon salt
4 white peppercorns

Place all the ingredients in a large pan and bring to the boil. Cover and simmer for 20 to 30 minutes. Strain and use to poach fish and shellfish.

Note: Part wine and part vinegar can be used, especially for strongly flavoured or oily fish such as mackerel.

Fumet de Poisson

Add the head, bones and trimmings from the fish to the court bouillon before simmering.

Halibut in rich tomato sauce

about 2 oz butter
1 onion, chopped
1 clove garlic, crushed
1 tablespoon tomato purée
1 teaspoon flour
5 fl oz dry white wine
15 oz can tomatoes
½ teaspoon Worcestershire sauce
½ teaspoon sugar
salt and freshly ground white pepper
4 halibut fillets
lemon wedges to garnish

Melt 1 oz butter in a saucepan and use to fry the onion and garlic until soft but not coloured. Add the tomato purée and flour and stir until well blended. Gradually add the wine and tomatoes and bring to the boil, stirring constantly. Add Worcestershire sauce and sugar, cover and simmer for about 10 minutes. Adjust seasoning. Meanwhile, place the fish in a grill pan, spread with butter and cook under medium heat for 5 to 8 minutes each side, depending on the thickness of the fillets. Place the cooked fish on a heated serving dish, pour the sauce over it and garnish with lemon wedges.

Halibut steaks in cognac sauce

1 strip lemon rind
2 cloves
1 small onion, sliced
$\frac{1}{4}$ teaspoon salt
small pinch white pepper
2 fl oz dry white wine
5 fl oz water
4 halibut steaks
4 lettuce leaves, shredded
2 tablespoons mayonnaise
1 tablespoon tomato ketchup
2 teaspoons tomato purée
2 tablespoons brandy
6 tablespoons double cream
1 lemon, sliced, 1 tablespoon capers, drained,
    and a few parsley sprigs to garnish

Place the lemon rind, cloves, onion and seasoning in a shallow pan with the wine and water. Bring to the boil then lower the fish gently into the pan, cover and simmer for 10 to 12 minutes, according to the thickness of the fish. Drain fish on absorbent kitchen paper, remove the skin and when completely cold arrange on a bed of lettuce. Lightly whip the cream and fold in the mayonnaise, ketchup,

tomato purée and brandy until well blended. Use to mask the fish steaks and garnish them with lemon slices, capers and parsley sprigs. Serve with tiny new boiled potatoes tossed in butter and chopped mint.

Cod Oporto

$1\frac{1}{2}$ lbs cod fillets or thin steaks
1 oz butter
salt
paprika
4 tablespoons port
2 tablespoons water
2 egg yolks
2 tablespoons cream

Lay the fish fillets in a buttered shallow ovenproof dish, season with salt and paprika and dot with the remaining butter. Bake in a moderate oven (350°F, 180°C, Gas Mark 4) for 5 minutes, add the port and water mixed, cover with greaseproof paper or foil and continue cooking for about 15 minutes until fish is opaque. Carefully strain off the liquor into a small saucepan and set aside to cool. Transfer the fish fillets to a warm serving dish, beat the egg yolks one at a time into the fish liquor, add the cream and reheat to just below simmering point, stirring constantly. Pour the sauce over the fish and serve with savoury rice.

Sole in champagne is the ultimate luxury; but if you allow for the sweetness in seasoning, German Sekt or Italian Asti could be used (my choice Kupferberg Gold or Asti Fontana).

Filets de sole au Muscadet

10 fl oz court bouillon (see page 63) made
    with Muscadet
4 large fillets of sole
3 egg yolks
1 tablespoon cream
1 oz Gruyère cheese, grated

Place the court bouillon in a shallow pan,
lower in the fillets and poach gently for 5
minutes. Drain the fish and place on a
heated serving dish. Boil the liquid hard
to reduce by half, strain, return to the pan
and bring back to the boil. Beat together
the egg yolks and cream. Add a little of
the hot liquid, beat well then return this
mixture to the pan and reheat gently
without boiling. Pour the sauce over the
fish, sprinkle with grated cheese and
brown quickly under a hot grill.

Turbot Aurore

5 fl oz dry white wine
3 oz butter, melted
4 turbot steaks
1 oz flour
10 fl oz milk
1 teaspoon anchovy essence
1 teaspoon tomato purée
salt and freshly ground black pepper
7¼ oz can shrimps, drained
2 tablespoons single cream

Boil the wine to reduce by half and allow
to cool. Melt 2 oz butter and use to brush
the fish steaks. Cook them under a
medium grill for about 15 minutes,
turning occasionally, until opaque. Meanwhile, melt the remaining butter in a
saucepan, stir in the flour and cook for 1
minute. Gradually add the milk and bring
to the boil, stirring constantly, until
smooth and thick. Add the anchovy
essence, reduced wine, tomato purée and
seasoning. Stir in the shrimps, heat
through, remove from heat and stir in the
cream. Remove the skin from the fish
steaks and place them on a heated serving
dish. Pour the sauce over and serve at once.

Simmered trout

6 small trout
salt and freshly ground black pepper
6 fl oz water
sauce:
1 small onion, finely chopped
1 small carrot, finely chopped
1¾ oz butter
12 fl oz red wine
½ oz flour
¼ teaspoon anchovy essence
1 teaspoon chopped fresh thyme
1 tablespoon chopped parsley
salt and freshly ground black pepper

Place the cleaned trout in a well buttered
ovenproof casserole. Sprinkle with seasoning and pour over the water. Cover
with foil and cook in a moderate oven
(350°F, 180°C, Gas Mark 4) for about 15
minutes. To make the sauce, heat ½ oz
butter in a pan and use to sauté the onion
and carrot until golden, then add the wine
and boil until reduced by half. Strain in
the liquor from cooking the trout and
bring to the boil. Make a beurre manié
with ¾ oz butter and the flour and add this
to the sauce in small pieces, stirring constantly until smooth. Simmer for 2
minutes then add the anchovy essence,
herbs and remaining butter. Taste and
adjust seasoning. Place trout on a heated
serving dish, pour the sauce over and
serve with boiled new potatoes.

Truite au vin rosé

4 trout
about 5 fl oz rosé wine
1 small onion, chopped
4 egg yolks
2½ oz butter
1 tablespoon lemon juice
salt and freshly ground white pepper
4 tablespoons double cream
croûtons or fleurons to garnish

Put the trout in a buttered baking dish, pour in the wine, arrange the onion round the fish and cover the dish with foil. Cook in a cool oven (300°F, 150°C, Gas Mark 2) for 20 minutes, or until the fish are cooked through. Drain on absorbent kitchen paper and remove the top skins. Keep warm. Boil the poaching liquid hard until reduced to 2 tablespoons. Put the egg yolks in a double boiler, strain in 1 tablespoon of the hot fish liquid and beat well. Add the remaining tablespoon of liquid and beat until slightly thickened. Remove the pan from the double boiler, beat in the butter in small pieces, and finally season to taste with the lemon juice, salt and pepper. Whip the cream lightly and fold into the sauce. Pour over the fish and garnish with fried bread croûtons.

Norwegian style trout

4 large trout
10 fl oz dry white wine
5 fl oz fish fumet (see page 63)
5 fl oz mayonnaise
2 oz shelled prawns
1 tablespoon capers, drained
1 tablespoon chopped gherkins
aspic jelly crystals to set 10 fl oz liquid
lemon slices to garnish

Have the fishmonger clean and bone the fish, but leave the heads on. Put the fish in a shallow pan with the wine and fish fumet and bring to the boil. Cover and simmer until fish are tender, about 8 minutes, then drain and cool. Blend the mayonnaise with the prawns, capers and gherkins and use to stuff the fish. Arrange on a serving platter. Dissolve the aspic jelly crystals in 10 fl oz measured from the strained fish liquor. Pour over the fish and allow to set. Garnish with lemon slices before serving.

Cold mullet with saffron

3 tablespoons oil
2 cloves garlic, crushed
6 8-oz mullet, gutted
20 fl oz dry white wine
4 tomatoes
good pinch powdered saffron
½ teaspoon dried thyme
¼ teaspoon ground bay leaves
6 sprigs parsley
salt and freshly ground black pepper
lemon slices to garnish

Heat the oil in a large shallow pan and use to fry the garlic until softened and golden. Add the fish and wine. Peel, remove seeds and chop the flesh of the tomatoes. Add to the pan with the saffron, thyme, ground bay leaves and parsley. Season lightly with salt and pepper. Bring to the boil, cover and simmer for 12 minutes. Remove fish to a shallow serving dish and cool. Boil the cooking liquid over high heat until reduced to one quarter, discard the parsley and allow to cool. Pour over the fish, garnish with lemon slices and serve cold.

Stuffed mackerel

2 tablespoons oil
4 small courgettes, sliced
1 clove garlic, crushed
1 tablespoon chopped parsley
1 teaspoon fennel seeds
salt and freshly ground black pepper
4 8-oz mackerel, gutted
5 fl oz dry white wine
½ oz butter
2 tablespoons dry white breadcrumbs

Heat the oil and use to sauté the courgettes and garlic gently until lightly browned. Add the parsley, fennel seeds and seasoning. Fill the cavities of the fish with this stuffing, place in a buttered baking dish and pour the wine over. Place uncovered in a moderate oven (350°F, 180°C, Gas Mark 4) for 25 minutes. Heat the butter, add the breadcrumbs and stir over heat until golden brown. Place the fish on a heated serving dish, boil the remaining fish liquid until reduced to 4 tablespoons, then strain over the fish. Spoon a layer of buttered crumbs over the fish to garnish.

Note: Stuffed fish can be spread with softened butter and baked *en papillote* wrapped in foil or greaseproof paper parcels, adding a little wine to the stuffing.

Mullet in a marinade

6 8-oz mullet, gutted
6 tablespoons oil
3 tablespoons dry white wine
salt and freshly ground black pepper
2 cloves garlic, chopped
1 tablespoon chopped oregano
1 tablespoon chopped parsley
3 tablespoons white wine vinegar
2 lemons, quartered

Make a few diagonal slits in the side of each of the fish and place in a shallow dish. Mix together 4 tablespoons of oil, the wine and seasoning and pour over the fish. Allow to marinade for at least 2 hours. Drain the fish and place them on the grid of a grill pan. Cook for 6 minutes on each side basting frequently with the marinade. Meanwhile, beat together the garlic, herbs, vinegar and remaining oil. Season with salt and pepper. Place the fish on a heated serving dish, garnish with lemon quarters and serve the cold sauce separately.

Note: It is essential to use fresh herbs to make this unusual cold sauce.

Vegetables

Vegetables cooked in wine? How odd, you may think. There are not many I would recommend but some are well worth trying. Sauerkraut, for me, takes on an entirely new and delicious aspect when gently bubbled in red wine and as for artichokes in white wine – sheer bliss.

Artichauts au vin blanc

4 globe artichokes
2 tablespoons oil
5 fl oz dry white wine
2 cloves garlic, crushed
1 small onion, chopped
1 tablespoon chopped parsley
salt and freshly ground white pepper

Trim the artichokes and remove chokes. Pull centre leaves apart, insert sharp knife between choke and base of artichoke, pull out the feathery choke. Combine the oil, wine, garlic, onion, parsley and seasoning to taste. Put the artichokes in a deep pan and pour the wine mixture over. Bring to the boil, cover and simmer for 45 minutes. Add a little more wine if the liquid boils down to less than half. Serve the artichokes with a little of the sauce poured over, or cold with a wine vinaigrette (see page 50).

Give class to tiny frozen vegetables by masking with savoury white sauce made as usual, with some well reduced white wine added.

Broccoli alla Romagna

7 tablespoons olive oil
2 cloves garlic, crushed
1½ lbs broccoli heads
salt and freshly ground black pepper
10 fl oz dry white wine

Heat the oil and use to sauté the garlic until golden. Add the broccoli heads, one at a time, and sauté for 4 to 5 minutes, stirring occasionally. Add seasoning to taste, the wine and just sufficient water to come through the vegetables. Bring to the boil, cover and cook for about 25 minutes, until the broccoli is just tender. Drain well, but reserve the cooking liquid for a sauce.

Note: Cauliflower florets may be cooked in the same way.

Sweet peppers alla Vittoria

2 tablespoons oil
1 small onion, finely chopped
1 clove garlic, crushed
4 medium tomatoes
1 tablespoon tomato purée
5 fl oz dry white wine
4 large red or green peppers
salt and freshly ground black pepper

Heat the oil and use it to sauté the onion and garlic until golden. Peel and chop the tomatoes and add to the pan with the tomato purée and wine. Cook for 3 minutes, stirring constantly. Deseed and slice the peppers. Add these to the pan and season to taste. Bring to the boil, cover and simmer gently for about 20 minutes, until the vegetables are tender.

Celery in Herb Sauce

Red cabbage with wine

2 oz butter
2 lbs red cabbage, shredded
1 onion, finely chopped
1 teaspoon salt
freshly ground black pepper
pinch grated nutmeg
2 cooking apples, grated
10 fl oz dry red wine

Melt the butter in a large pan, add the cabbage and toss until well coated. Add the onion to the pan with the salt, pepper to taste, the nutmeg, apple and wine. Stir well, bring to the boil, cover and simmer gently for about 50 minutes, until cabbage is tender.

Poireaux à l'indienne

1½ lbs young leeks, trimmed
2 tablespoons oil
5 fl oz dry white wine
juice of ½ lemon
2 teaspoons curry powder
salt
pinch cayenne
1 teaspoon dried mixed herbs
1 bay leaf
10 fl oz water
1 large onion, chopped

Remove all the green part of the leeks and use up for soup. Cut the leeks into 1½ inch lengths and wash well. Put the oil, white wine, lemon juice, curry powder, salt, cayenne, herbs and bay leaf in a saucepan with the water. Boil, uncovered, for 5 minutes, add the leeks and onion and cook, uncovered, until the leeks are tender. Serve with pork or lamb, or cold as a light main dish.

Celery in herb sauce

2 heads celery
2 oz butter
2 teaspoons chopped parsley
1 teaspoon chopped tarragon
5 fl oz dry white wine
salt and freshly ground white pepper
½ chicken stock cube
5 fl oz boiling water

Clean and chop the celery roughly, removing strings from large stalks, and cook in boiling salted water, for 20 minutes. Drain and arrange in a buttered shallow ovenproof dish. Meanwhile make the sauce. Simmer the herbs gently, uncovered, in the wine. Season to taste. Pour over the celery. Make up the stock cube with the boiling water and pour over the celery. Dot with remaining butter and cook in a moderate oven (350°F, 180°C, Gas Mark 4) for 30 minutes.

Main dishes

Meat, poultry, game; all are tenderized, enriched, enhanced by the warm kiss of red or white wine. Even the tasteless turkey, a bird I can only enjoy whole-heartedly through a haze of Christmas cheer, gains excitement. My favourite zip-up for turkey is to use wine in the sauce *and* the stuffing. Reheated food is a bore to most people; to me it is a challenge. 'My Moussaka' resulted from a triumphant encounter with half a leg of roast lamb which had to be transformed willy nilly into a dish to serve four guests. Swiss cheese soufflé has crept into this section, on the grounds that if you have *nothing* available to reheat, you are more likely to have cheese in the house than any other staple protein food.

Smyrna kebabs

1 lb boned leg of lamb, diced
8 oz button mushrooms, halved
1 large aubergine, diced
honey marinade (see page 60)

Put the meat, mushrooms and aubergine in a bowl, cover with the marinade and leave to stand for at least 2 hours. Thread the lamb onto skewers, alternating with the mushrooms and aubergine dice. Place loaded skewers under a hot grill, brush with the marinade and cook, turning several times, for 8 to 10 minutes, basting frequently with the remaining marinade.

Roast lamb with red wine jelly

3–4 lb leg of lamb
2 oz butter
1 teaspoon dried rosemary
2 tablespoons red wine
red wine jelly:
11 oz can mandarin oranges
5 fl oz red wine
1 oz caster sugar
good pinch ground ginger
1 tablespoon gelatine
few drops red food colouring

To make the jelly, drain the mandarins and make up the syrup with the wine and sufficient water to make 10 fl oz. Soften the gelatine in 2 tablespoons cold water. Place the wine mixture in a saucepan with the sugar and ginger and bring to the boil. Stir the softened gelatine into the hot liquid, add red food colouring if desired and pour this into a shallow dish to make a layer about half an inch deep. Leave in a cool place until set. Weigh the joint. Beat together the butter and rosemary then gradually add the wine, a little at a time beating continuously. Smear this mixture over the joint and place in a roasting tin. Roast in a moderately hot oven (400°F, 200°C, Gas Mark 6) for 30 minutes per pound, basting once with the juices in pan. Meanwhile stamp out small shapes from the jelly with a fancy cutter and remove with a warm palette knife dipped in hot water and shaken dry. Place the roast joint on a serving dish and surround with jelly shapes, each topped with a mandarin orange segment. Make a thick brown sauce with the pan juices and stir in any surplus jelly trimmings. Bring to boiling point and serve separately.

Swiss cheese soufflé

aspic jelly crystals to set 15 fl oz liquid
2 tablespoons hot water
10 fl oz dry white wine
3 eggs, separated
5 fl oz double cream
5 fl oz single cream
salt and freshly ground white pepper
4 oz Gruyère cheese, grated
2 oz Emmenthal cheese, grated
2 tablespoons chopped parsley

Prepare a 30 fl oz soufflé dish by fixing a paper cuff round it with an elastic band to stand up at least 2 inches above the top of the dish. Oil the inside of the cuff lightly. Dissolve the aspic jelly crystals in the water. Place in the top of a double boiler with the wine and egg yolks. Whisk over moderate heat until foamy and beginning to coat the whisk. Remove from the heat and allow to cool. Meanwhile in a clean basin beat the double cream until it forms peaks, then beat in the single cream and seasoning gradually. When the aspic mixture is becoming syrupy, fold this into the cream with the grated cheese. Beat the egg whites until stiff and fold in. Pour into the prepared soufflé dish and chill until set. Strip off the paper cuff and press chopped parsley against the exposed sides of the soufflé to coat it. Serve chilled. Alternatively, it is less trouble to pour the mixture into 6 miniature soufflé dishes, and when set, coat with another thin layer of aspic.

Serve eggs poached in dry white wine on buttered toast as a light meal. Reduce poaching liquid to 1 tablespoon per egg, pour over.

Barbecued rack of lamb

4 racks of lamb, each weighing about 1 lb
2 cloves garlic, crushed
4 tablespoons oil
3 tablespoons soy sauce
3 tablespoons dry white wine
salt and freshly ground black pepper

Ask the butcher to cut you four sections from the best end of neck of small lambs, for roasting. Each rack should have four bones, and be chined. Mix together the garlic, oil, soy sauce, wine and seasoning to taste. Rub the mixture into the lamb and allow to stand for about 2 hours. Put the meat into a large roasting tin and roast in a moderate oven (350°F, 180°C, Gas Mark 4) for 40 to 45 minutes, according to size, basting several times with any remaining wine marinade. Serve the meat, still slightly pink, with tiny young vegetables.

Creamy lamb curry

2 lbs best end of neck noisettes of lamb
fat for frying
2 onions, chopped
1 tablespoon curry powder
2 tablespoons flour
5 fl oz double cream
5 fl oz dry white wine
40 fl oz stock
salt
1 cooking apple
2 tablespoons desiccated coconut

Place the noisettes in a large pan and fry until browned all over. Remove to an ovenproof casserole. Add a little fat to the

Lamb Cutlets en Croute

pan if necessary and use to fry the onion until golden. Stir in the curry powder and flour until well blended. Gradually add the cream, wine and stock and bring to the boil, stirring constantly, until the sauce is smooth and thickened. Season with salt. Peel, core and chop the apple, add to the sauce with the coconut and pour over the meat. Cover and cook in a moderate oven (350°F, 180°C, Gas Mark 4) for 1½ hours.

Fresh lamb Moussaka

oil for frying
2 large onions, sliced
1½ lbs minced raw lamb
2 large tomatoes, skinned
½ teaspoon grated nutmeg
½ teaspoon ground cinnamon
2 tablespoons chopped parsley
salt and freshly ground black pepper
5 fl oz red wine
1 lb potatoes
1 large aubergine
topping:
3 oz butter
4 tablespoons flour
20 fl oz warm milk
pinch grated nutmeg
1 oz grated parmesan cheese
salt and freshly ground black pepper
2 eggs, beaten

Heat a little oil and use to fry the onion slices until soft. Add the meat and cook stirring until browned. Chop the tomatoes and add to the pan with the nutmeg, cinnamon, parsley and seasoning. Mix well and moisten with the wine. Bring to the boil, cover and simmer for 20 minutes. Meanwhile peel the potatoes and aubergine and slice thinly. Fry the slices in plenty of oil in a large frying pan, until they are brown on both sides. To make the topping, in a clean pan melt the butter and stir in the flour. Gradually add the warm milk and bring to the boil, stirring constantly. Cook for 2 minutes and add the nutmeg, cheese and seasoning. Mix 2 tablespoons sauce with the meat mixture and arrange alternate layers of the potatoes and meat mixture in a baking tin or shallow earthenware ovenproof casserole, finishing with a layer of potato and aubergine. Add the well beaten eggs to the sauce and pour over the top of the casserole. Cook in a moderately hot oven (375°F, 190°C, Gas Mark 5) for about 45 minutes, until the top is golden brown.

Cotelettes d'agneau soubise

2 best ends of neck of lamb, divided into 10–12
    cutlets
1 oz butter
8 oz onion, sliced
1 bay leaf
5 fl oz dry white wine
salt and freshly ground white pepper to taste
10 fl oz béchamel sauce, hot
pinch caster sugar
1 lb creamy mashed potato
paprika

Trim the cutlets neatly, heat the butter and brown the cutlets all over. Remove and keep hot. Add the onion to the pan and sauté until pale golden. Return the cutlets to the pan, add bay leaf, white wine and seasoning. Cover and simmer gently for 20 minutes. Remove cutlets to a heated serving dish, discard bay leaf, purée the contents of the pan and mix into the hot béchamel sauce with the sugar. Pour sauce over the cutlets and serve in a border of mashed potato, with paprika.

Escalopes 'Roi René'

4 escalopes of veal
salt and freshly ground white pepper
1 oz fat or oil
5 fl oz stock
1 teaspoon cornflour
2 teaspoons Cointreau
orange slices to garnish

Beat the escalopes thinly and rub in seasoning. Heat the fat and use to brown the escalopes on both sides. Remove from the pan and place on a heated serving dish. Add the stock to the juices in the pan. Moisten the cornflour with a little cold water and add to the stock. Bring to the boil, stirring constantly. Add the liqueur, pour over the escalopes and garnish with orange slices.

Veal Stroganoff

1½ lb leg of veal
1½ oz lard or dripping
salt and freshly ground white pepper
1 oz butter
1 tablespoon chopped onion
2 tablespoons flour
pinch curry powder
5 fl oz dry white wine
10 fl oz chicken stock
4 oz button mushrooms
10 fl oz single cream

Cut the veal into neat strips. Melt the lard and use to sauté the strips until golden, then cook gently until the juices begin to run. Season to taste, remove veal from the pan and keep hot. In a clean pan melt the butter and use to cook the onion until pale gold. Stir in the flour and curry powder and cook for 1 minute. Add the wine, stock and mushrooms and bring to the boil, stirring constantly. Add the stock and cook until sauce is reduced by half. Add the pan juices from cooking the meat and the cooked veal strips. Stir in the cream and reheat gently without boiling.

Roast veal with herbs and cream

1 shoulder of veal (3–3½ lbs), boned
1 oz butter
1 tablespoon oil
1 small onion, very finely chopped
salt and freshly ground white pepper
¼ teaspoon dried oregano
5 fl oz dry white wine
5 fl oz double cream

Tie the meat into a neat shape and place in a roasting tin. Heat together the butter and oil and use to fry the onion until softened, then stir in seasonings, herbs and wine. Bring to the boil. Pour this over the meat in the roasting tin and roast in a hot oven (425°F, 220°C, Gas Mark 7) for 30 minutes per pound and 30 minutes over, basting frequently. Remove joint, slice thickly and place on a heated serving dish. Keep hot. Add the cream to the juices in the pan and stir well. Simmer for 3 minutes then pour over the veal.

Meat can be cooked from the frozen state but if you prefer not to, make a virtue of necessity. Prepare a marinade, and defrost the meat in this, tenderising and improving the flavour at the same time. Turn the meat often.

Choucroûte Alsacienne

5 fl oz Riesling or other dry white wine
2 bay leaves
2 lbs sauerkraut
1 oz flour
1 oz butter, melted
2 teaspoons sugar
8 oz boiled salt belly of pork, sliced
8 oz boiled gammon, sliced
8 oz frankfurter sausages

Place the wine in a small saucepan with the bay leaves and boil until reduced by half. Put the sauerkraut into an ovenproof casserole. Mix together the flour and melted butter until smooth. Add the reduced wine and the sugar and mix well. Stir this into the sauerkraut, cover and place in a moderately hot oven (400°F, 200°C, Gas Mark 6) for 5 minutes. Arrange the cooked meat and sausages on the bed of sauerkraut, cover and return to the oven for 30 minutes. Serve with boiled potatoes.

Note: In Alsace this is usually served with pease pudding as well as boiled potatoes.

Münchener sauerkraut

2 oz lard
2 onions, sliced
1 cooking apple
¼ teaspoon dried thyme
1 teaspoon caraway seeds
1 bay leaf
freshly ground black pepper
20 fl oz dry white wine
2 lb sauerkraut
4 oz smoked bacon
4 oz unsmoked bacon
1 lb frankfurter sausages
gherkins to garnish

Melt the lard in a flameproof casserole and use to fry the onion until brown. Peel and grate the apple and add to the pan with the herbs, bay leaf, pepper and wine. Cook for 5 minutes. Add the sauerkraut and bacon. Cook for 5 minutes. Add the sauerkraut and bacon. Bring to the boil, cover and simmer for 30 minutes. Add the pork, recover and cook for about 2 hours, until tender, adding the frankfurters 10 minutes before the end of cooking time. Garnish with gherkins.

Tipsy gammon

3 lb corner gammon joint
sauce:
1 tablespoon prepared mustard
2 teaspoons Worcestershire sauce
7 fl oz dry red wine
1 teaspoon salt
1 teaspoon freshly ground pepper
glaze:
3 tablespoons demerara sugar

Place the gammon in a deep pan, cover with water and bring slowly to boiling point. Cover and simmer gently for 50 minutes. Drain joint, strip off skin and score fat layer neatly into 'diamonds'. Place joint in a roasting tin. Combine all ingredients for the sauce and beat well together. Spoon over joint. Place in a moderately hot oven (375°F, 190°C, Gas Mark 5) for about 30 minutes, basting once with the sauce during this time. Pour off sauce. Heat 2 tablespoons of the demerara sugar in 4 tablespoons of the sauce until dissolved, boil rapidly for 1 minute, pour over the scored fat, sprinkle with the remaining sugar and return to the oven for 10 minutes, or place under a hot grill for 3 minutes. Serve with Kerry Baked Potatoes.

Tipsy Gammon with Kerry-baked Potatoes

Kerrybaked potatoes

2 lbs floury potatoes
4 oz butter
salt and freshly ground white pepper
5 fl oz single cream

Peel and slice the potatoes thickly. Arrange in a well buttered shallow casserole, over-lapping in layers. Sprinkle each layer with salt, pepper, dot with butter and a little of the cream. Continue until all ingredients are used up, ending with a layer of cream. Cover lightly with foil and cook in a moderate oven (350°F, 180°C, Gas Mark 4) for 40 minutes. Remove foil and return to the oven for a further 10 to 15 minutes.

Note: If waxy potatoes are used, parboil slices in salted water for 2 minutes.

Ham in redcurrant sauce

2 oz butter
6 thick slices gammon
1 tablespoon plain flour
10 fl oz dry white wine
3 tablespoons redcurrant jelly
1 teaspoon mustard
salt and freshly ground white pepper
1 lb mashed potatoes
1 egg, beaten
¼ teaspoon grated nutmeg
little milk

Melt the butter and use to fry the gammon slices on both sides until brown (about 5 minutes). Remove gammon and stir flour into the juices in the pan. Gradually add the wine, redcurrant jelly and mustard and bring to the boil, stirring constantly. Taste and add salt and pepper only if necessary. Beat the potato until smooth then add the egg and nutmeg and beat

again. Add sufficient milk to give a creamy consistency and pile the potato in the centre of a heated serving dish. Surround with the gammon slices and pour the sauce over these.

Filet de porc en croûte

1 tablespoon corn oil
4 tablespoons dry white wine
½ teaspoon salt
¼ teaspoon freshly ground black pepper
1 large pork fillet
2 oz long grain rice
2 oz butter
4 oz mushrooms, sliced
2 oz lean ham, diced
12 oz puff pastry, chilled
1 egg, beaten

Mix together the oil, wine, salt and pepper. Pour this over the neatly trimmed fillet in a shallow dish. Allow to marinate for several hours, turning occasionally, then drain well. Place fillet on a baking sheet and put in a hot oven (425°F, 220°C, Gas Mark 7) for 5 minutes to seal. Meanwhile, cook and drain the rice. Melt the butter and use to sauté the mushrooms lightly. Stir in the remaining marinade, ham and rice. Roll out the pastry to a rectangle three inches longer than the fillet and three times as wide. Cut off a 1-inch strip for decoration. Spread some of the rice mixture down the centre of the pastry and place the sealed fillet on this. Spread the rest of the rice mixture over the fillet and turn in the ends of the pastry. Brush all edges with beaten egg, bring the sides up, seal together on top and decorate with three narrow plaited strips or diamond-shaped pastry leaves. Brush again with egg, transfer to a damped baking sheet and bake in a hot oven (425°F, 220°C,

Gas Mark 7) for 25 minutes, or until golden brown. Serve with a crisp green salad.

Camper's feast

1 oz butter
1½ lbs pork and beef sausages (or either kind)
2 tablespoons dry white breadcrumbs
10 fl oz robust red wine
good pinch dried mixed herbs
salt and freshly ground black pepper

Melt just enough butter in a strong frying pan to start cooking the sausages without allowing them to stick. Keep turning over moderate heat until they are light golden brown all over. Add the breadcrumbs, increase heat and keep stirring gently until the crumbs are golden brown. Add the wine, bring just to the boil, add the herbs and seasoning and simmer uncovered for 7 to 8 minutes.

Note: I have seen this made by French campers many a time. All experienced campers bring polythene bags of ready-grated cheese and dry breadcrumbs too, sufficient for the holiday.

Pork paprika

2 lbs fillet of pork
salt and freshly ground white pepper
1½ oz butter
1 tablespoon oil
1 onion, sliced
2 tablespoons paprika
15 fl oz dry white wine
10 fl oz chicken stock
1 tablespoon flour
10 fl oz soured cream

Cut the meat into narrow strips and season with salt and pepper. Heat the butter and oil in a large frying pan and use to cook the meat gently until pale golden. Add the onion and continue to cook until softened and just coloured. Remove pan from heat, add the paprika and stir well. Add the wine gradually, replace over heat and cook until almost all the liquid has evaporated. Pour in the stock and stir round well. Mix together the flour and cream, stir this into the pan and reheat to just below boiling point. Cover and simmer for a further 10 minutes until slightly thickened. Adjust seasoning and serve with buttered rice.

Pork in mild mustard sauce

8 oz lean gammon rashers
1 onion, chopped
12 fl oz dry white wine
salt and freshly ground white pepper
4 lean pork chops
1 oz plain flour
2 oz butter
5 fl oz double cream
1 teaspoon mild continental mustard
1 tablespoon chopped parsley

Remove the rind and cut the gammon rashers into strips. Place these in a shallow dish, sprinkle with the chopped onion and pour over the wine. Leave in a cool place for 1 hour. Season the chops and coat them in flour. Heat the butter and use to fry the chops gently for 5 to 7 minutes on each side. Add the drained onions and gammon strips and continue cooking for 2 to 3 minutes. Pour in the wine and the cream and simmer for 10 to 12 minutes. Place the chops on a heated serving dish, reduce the sauce slightly by boiling, stir in the mustard and adjust seasoning. Spoon the sauce over the chops and sprinkle with parsley.

Filet de porc à l'orange

2 oz butter
4 carrots, sliced
2 lbs pork fillet
knuckle of veal
2 tablespoons brandy
10 fl oz dry white wine
½ teaspoon dried thyme
1 bay leaf
salt and freshly ground white pepper
3 oranges
orange slices to garnish

Melt the butter and use to fry the carrots gently until slightly softened. Put in the fillet and brown all over. Add the veal bone and cook for a further 2 to 3 minutes. Pour the brandy into a ladle or small pan, warm slightly, ignite and pour over the meat. When the flames have subsided, pour in the wine and add the herbs, bay leaf and seasoning. Bring to the boil, cover and simmer gently for an hour, or until tender. Remove the pork and keep hot. Skim surplus fat from the pan and strain the sauce through a fine sieve. Finely grate the zest from the oranges and squeeze the juice. Add both to the sauce and bring to the boil. Serve the pork sliced in the sauce and garnish with thin slices of fresh orange.

Taverner's steak

4 rump steaks
salt and freshly ground black pepper
2 oz butter
1 tablespoon oil
5 fl oz full-bodied red wine
1 tablespoon chopped parsley
4 lemon wedges to garnish

Trim the steaks and season with salt and pepper. Heat the butter and oil together in a frying pan and use to cook the steaks quickly until the juices appear on the surface; turn them over and cook other side. Place steaks on a heated serving dish and keep hot. To the juices in the pan add the wine and boil hard, scraping up the sediment, until reduced by about half. Adjust seasoning. Serve the steaks with the sauce poured over, garnished with chopped parsley and lemon wedges.

The Dean's beef pie

2 tablespoons dripping
1½ lbs braising steak, cubed
6 oz ox kidney, cubed
1 onion, chopped
1 tablespoon flour
5 fl oz red wine
5 fl oz beef stock
½ teaspoon dried oregano
salt and freshly ground black pepper
4 oz button mushrooms, sliced
8 oz puff pastry
1 egg, beaten

Melt the dripping in a frying pan and use to fry the steak and kidney cubes until browned. Remove them to an ovenproof casserole and then add the onion to the fat remaining in the pan. Cook until browned then stir in the flour until blended. Gradually add the wine and stock and bring to the boil, stirring constantly. Add the herbs and season to taste. Pour over the beef, cover and cook in a moderate oven (350°F, 180°C, Gas Mark 4) for an hour. Turn into a 40 fl oz pie dish and stir in the mushrooms. Roll out the pastry and use to cover the pie, then use the trimmings to decorate. Brush with beaten egg. Raise oven heat to hot (425°F, 220°C,

Gas Mark 7). Return pie to oven for 20 minutes, then reduce heat to moderately hot again and continue cooking for a further 20 minutes, protecting top of pastry with a sheet of foil if necessary to prevent over-browning.

Badischer sauerbraten

joint topside of beef (3–4 lbs)
20 fl oz cooked red wine marinade (see page 60)
4 whole allspice berries
½ lemon, sliced
3 oz butter
2 oz flour
1 tablespoon brown sugar

The meat should be neatly tied and placed in a deep bowl. Make the marinade, and add the allspice berries and the lemon slices. Pour it boiling over the meat, cover the bowl and allow to stand in a cool place for 2 to 3 days, turning each day. Remove joint from the marinade and wipe dry. Melt 2 oz of the butter in a flameproof casserole and use to seal the meat on all sides. Sprinkle in half the flour and brown well. Reheat the marinade and strain over the meat. Bring to the boil, cover tightly and simmer for 2 to 3 hours, or until the meat is tender. Pour off the stock and skim off surplus fat. Melt remaining butter in a clean saucepan and stir in the rest of the flour until well blended. Add the sugar and stir until light brown. Add the stock gradually and bring to boiling point, stirring constantly, until sauce is thick and smooth. Slice the meat thickly, place on a heated serving dish and pour the sauce over. This dish may be accompanied by boiled potatoes or noodles.

Note: No other authentic recipe for Sauerbraten I know includes red wine.

But as Baden is one of the few regions in Germany which produces red wine, this is understandable.

Wine glazed chicken portions

8 chicken portions
2 oz unsalted butter
5 tablespoons clear honey
1 tablespoon soy sauce
5 fl oz dry red wine
salt and freshly ground white pepper
12 oz long grain rice
7 oz can red pimiento
8 oz cooked peas, hot
1 lb cooked asparagus spears, hot

Mix together the softened butter, honey and soy sauce. Use to brush the chicken portions and lay side by side in a roasting tin, skin side down. Pour the wine into the roasting tin and place in a hot oven (425°F, 220°C, Gas Mark 7) for 35 minutes. Half way through the cooking time turn the chicken portions, sprinkle with salt and pepper, and baste occasionally with the juices in the pan. Meanwhile, cook the rice in plenty of boiling salted water until just tender, drain well in a colander or sieve and pour fresh boiling water through it. Shake it as dry as possible. Drain and chop the red pimiento finely, reserving a few strips for the garnish. Lightly fork the juice from the can into the rice together with the hot peas and chopped pimiento. Pile up in the centre of a large heated serving dish and surround with the glazed chicken portions. Reduce the juices in the pan slightly and spoon over the chicken portions to build up the glaze. Arrange small piles of asparagus spears, garnished with the pimiento strips, between the chicken portions. (Serves 8.)

Lemon chicken fricassée

1 chicken stock cube
15 fl oz boiling water
2 carrots
8 small onions
bouquet garni
4 chicken portions
salt and freshly ground white pepper
2 oz butter
5 fl oz white wine
4 tablespoons lemon juice
2 egg yolks

Make up the stock cube with the boiling water and place in a saucepan with the carrots, onions and bouquet garni. Add the chicken portions, bring to the boil, cover and simmer for 20 minutes. Remove chicken and pat dry on absorbent kitchen paper. Strain the stock and adjust seasoning. Heat the butter and use to fry the chicken pieces until pale golden. Add wine and sufficient stock to cover. Bring to the boil and cook for 5 minutes. Remove chicken to a heated serving dish. Beat together the lemon juice and egg yolks, stir in a little of the hot wine stock. Add the egg yolk mixture to the pan and stir well. Remove from heat and pour over the chicken. Serve with rice.

Poulet en chemise aux pois

1 red pepper
2 oz butter
4 oz button mushrooms
1 lb cooked white chicken meat, diced
salt and freshly ground white pepper
5 fl oz cream
2 egg yolks
6 tablespoons sherry

Deseed and slice the red pepper. Melt the butter in a saucepan, add mushrooms and pepper slices, cover and cook gently for 5 minutes. Add the chicken and seasoning and reheat. Mix together 2 tablespoons cream and the egg yolks. Stir the sherry and remaining cream into the chicken mixture, when hot add the egg yolk mixture and reheat until thickened but do not allow to boil. Serve with rice.

Dijon chicken

2 oz butter
4 chicken portions
7 tablespoons dry white wine
bouquet garni
salt and freshly ground white pepper
2 egg yolks
2 tablespoons soured cream
2 tablespoons Dijon mustard
pinch cayenne

Melt the butter and use to fry the chicken portions until browned on all sides. Add the wine, bouquet garni and seasoning and bring to the boil. Cover and simmer gently for 25 minutes. Remove chicken to a heated serving dish. Discard the bouquet garni. Mix together the egg yolks, cream, mustard and cayenne. Stir this into the gravy and reheat, stirring, until the sauce thickens, but do not allow it to boil. Pour sauce over the chicken.

Sweet pepper chicken

4 chicken portions
salt and freshly ground white pepper
3 oz butter
3 rashers streaky bacon, chopped
6 tomatoes
1 red pepper
2 large onions
7 tablespoons port

Rub the chicken with salt and pepper. Melt the butter in a large flameproof casserole, add the bacon and cook until browned. Add the chicken portions and continue cooking until they are golden on both sides. Meanwhile, peel, deseed and chop the tomatoes, deseed and chop the pepper and slice the onions thinly. Add all these to the casserole with the port. Bring to the boil, cover and cook gently until the chicken is tender and vegetables cooked. Serve on buttered rice.

Poulet aux fonds d'artichauts

5 fl oz dry white wine
10 fl oz hot béchamel sauce
8 canned artichoke bottoms
1 lb cooked white chicken meat, diced
1 egg yolk
5 fl oz single cream
1 hard boiled egg
fried bread croûtons to garnish

Stir the wine into the hot béchamel sauce and cook until reduced by about one quarter. Chop four of the artichoke bottoms and add to the sauce with the chicken and heat through. Beat together the egg yolk and cream, add to the sauce and stir until thickened but do not allow to boil. Place in a heated serving dish. Halve the hard boiled egg and scoop out the yolk from both halves. Press the yolk through a sieve over the surface of the blanquette. Heat the remaining artichoke bottoms in the liquid from the can. Serve portions of the blanquette with an artichoke bottom on each filled with fried bread croûtons and chopped egg white.

Suprèmes de volaille au muscadet

8 boned chicken breasts
salt and freshly ground white pepper
4 oz butter
1 lb pâté de foie gras
5 fl oz muscadet
20 fl oz béchamel sauce
5 fl oz double cream
sprigs of watercress to garnish

Remove skin from chicken breasts and flatten them. Season with salt and pepper. Melt the butter and use to fry the chicken gently for 15 minutes until tender but not coloured. Cut the pâté into 8 slices and place on a heated serving dish. Top each slice with a chicken breast and keep hot. Pour the muscadet into the remaining butter in the pan and stir over high heat for 2 minutes. Gradually stir in the béchamel sauce and bring to boiling point. Stir in the cream and pour sauce over the chicken. Garnish with sprigs of watercress.

Duck in pineapple glaze

4 portions duck
1 tablespoon oil
salt and freshly ground black pepper
5 fl oz red wine
8 oz can pineapple rings
1 orange
1 tablespoon cornflour

Arrange the duck portions, skin side up, in a roasting tin, brush lightly with oil and sprinkle with salt and pepper. Mix together the wine and the syrup from the can of pineapple. Pour this round the duck. Cook in a moderately hot oven (375°F, 190°C, Gas Mark 5) for 45 minutes, basting several times with the juices in the pan. Remove the duck portions to a heated serving dish. Skim off surplus fat from the roasting tin. Grate the zest from the orange and reserve, squeeze the juice and use to moisten the cornflour. Add the cornflour to the pan and bring to the boil, stirring constantly until thick and smooth. Place the pineapple rings in the sauce and heat through. Place a pineapple ring on each duck portion, strain the sauce over and garnish with a sprinkling of orange zest.

Roast duck with Seville sauce

1 large duck (about 5 lbs)
1 orange
1 tablespoon cornflour
7 tablespoons port
2 teaspoons marmalade
pinch ground allspice
salt and freshly ground black pepper
watercress to garnish

Place the duck on a trivet in a roasting pan and roast in a moderately hot oven (400°F, 200°C, Gas Mark 6) for 2 hours. Remove duck to a heated serving dish. Meanwhile finely grate zest from orange and squeeze the juice. Remove surplus fat from pan and stir in the cornflour until well blended. Gradually stir in the port, orange zest and juice, marmalade and allspice. Bring to the boil, stirring constantly and cook for 2 minutes. Adjust seasoning. Garnish the duck with watercress and serve the sauce separately.

Caneton aux pêches

2 ducklings or 1 duck (4–5 lbs)
salt and freshly ground black pepper
1 onion, sliced
1 carrot, sliced
bouquet garni
2 tablespoons brandy
2 tablespoons Curaçao
1 tablespoon cornflour
4 large peaches

Place the giblets in a saucepan with seasoning, onion, carrot, bouquet garni and water to cover and simmer to make stock. Stand ducklings or duck on a trivet in a roasting pan and roast in a moderately hot oven (400°F, 200°C, Gas Mark 6) for 15 minutes per pound and 45 minutes over. Remove from oven and place on a heated serving dish. Keep hot. Drain surplus fat from roasting tin, keeping the juices. Into these pour the brandy and Curaçao and boil hard, scraping up the sediment. Moisten the cornflour with a little cold water and stir into the pan with 10 fl oz strained giblet stock. Bring to the boil, stirring constantly. Peel, halve and remove stones from peaches. Place these in the sauce and simmer for 5 minutes. Adjust seasoning. Place peaches round the ducklings and serve the sauce separately.

A sauce to put roast duck in the gourmet class is made by removing surplus fat from the pan, using juices plus gravy powder, water from vegetables, 2 tablespoons dry sherry.

Dindonneau à la crème

4 raw turkey breast slices
salt and freshly ground white pepper
3 oz butter
1 tablespoon flour
5 fl oz dry white wine
4 oz button mushrooms
15 fl oz double cream
1 tablespoon chopped parsley to garnish

Season the turkey slices with salt and pepper. Melt the butter and use to sauté these until light golden on both sides, then remove. Stir the flour into the juices in the pan until well blended. Add the wine gradually and bring to the boil, stirring constantly. Put the turkey slices back in, add the mushrooms and bring to the boil. Cover and simmer for 30 minutes. Place turkey slices on a heated serving dish. Blend the cream into the sauce, reheat without boiling and pour over the turkey. Sprinkle with chopped parsley before serving.

Roast turkey with wine sauce and stuffing

1 small turkey (6–8 lbs) – if frozen, fully
  defrosted
2 sticks celery
3 oz butter
2 oz bacon, diced
1 bottle full-bodied red wine
6 oz soft white breadcrumbs
2 oz walnuts, finely chopped
salt and freshly ground pepper
1 lightly beaten egg
4 tablespoons stock
1 tablespoon oil
1 chicken stock cube
$\frac{3}{4}$ oz flour

Chop the celery finely and fry lightly in 2 oz of the butter with the bacon until the celery is soft but not coloured. Add 5 fl oz of the wine and boil rapidly to reduce by half. Stir in the breadcrumbs, walnuts and seasoning to taste. Bind with the lightly beaten egg and sufficient stock to make a good firm stuffing consistency. Use to stuff the neck cavity of the turkey. Brush the bird lightly with oil, sprinkle with salt and pepper and place in a large roasting bag. Put the bag in a roasting tin in a moderately hot oven (375°F, 190°C, Gas Mark 5) for $2\frac{1}{2}$ to 3 hours, depending on weight. Strain the clear stock from the bag into a measuring jug, add the stock cube and make up to 15 fl oz with more of the wine. Cook the remaining butter and the flour together until nut brown. Gradually stir in the wine stock and cook, stirring constantly, until thick and smooth. Adjust seasoning to taste. Place the turkey on a heated serving dish and serve the sauce separately.

Pheasant with apples and raisins

3 oz seedless raisins
6 tablespoons white wine
3 oz butter
1 young roasting pheasant
$1\frac{1}{2}$ lbs dessert apples
pinch cinnamon
7 tablespoons cream
juice of $\frac{1}{2}$ lemon
2 tablespoons Calvados or brandy
salt and freshly ground black pepper

Soak the raisins in the wine for 2 hours. Melt 1 oz butter in a flameproof casserole. Put in the pheasant and turn it in the hot fat until golden brown all over, then

Roast Turkey with Wine Sauce
and Stuffing

remove. Peel and core the apples and cut them in thin slices. Heat the remaining butter in another pan, add apple slices and fry over a high heat to brown without cooking. Put half the apple slices in the casserole, put the pheasant on these and surround with the remaining apple slices. Sprinkle with cinnamon. Mix together the cream, lemon juice and Calvados and add salt and pepper to taste. Pour this over the pheasant and sprinkle over the raisins and their soaking liquid. Cover and simmer for 45 minutes.

Faisan à la vigneronne

---

4 oz white grapes
1 tablespoon dry sherry
1 tablespoon brandy (optional)
1 oz butter
1 young pheasant
1 large slice fat bacon
4 oz crescent shaped croûtons to garnish
bunch watercress to garnish

Peel the grapes and place in a small dish. Pour over them the sherry and brandy (if used). Put the butter inside the bird, cover the breast with the bacon and roast in a moderately hot oven (400°F, 200°C, Gas Mark 6) for 30 minutes. Remove bacon, baste the bird and strain the liquid from the grapes over it. Return to the oven, basting frequently until the bird is cooked, about 15 minutes. Transfer to a warm serving dish. Reduce the juice in the roasting pan over a high heat by about half and strain over the bird. Garnish with the croûtons, grapes and watercress.

Older game birds too tough to roast are delicious if braised on a bed of diced vegetables with red wine.

Perdreaux à deux

---

2 young partridges
1 lb white grapes
4 oz green bacon
salt and freshly ground black pepper
2 oz butter
2 slices white bread
1 tablespoon oil
4 tablespoons white wine

Clean the partridges and stuff them with a few whole grapes. Place the remaining grapes in a bowl and crush them. Squeeze out as much juice as possible either by putting through a fruit press or placing in a piece of muslin and wringing this over a bowl. Derind the bacon. Season the partridges, wrap in bacon spread with half the butter and place in a roasting tin. Roast in a hot oven (425°F, 220°C, Gas Mark 7) for 25 to 30 minutes. Cut the bread slices into rounds the same size as the partridges. Heat together the remaining butter and the oil in a frying pan and use to fry the bread until golden on both sides. Place croûtes on a heated serving dish and put a partridge on each. Keep hot. Into the juices in the roasting pan pour the grape juice and the wine. Bring to the boil, and boil for 10 minutes, or until reduced by half. Strain over partridges.

Saddle of hare in Madeira sauce

---

1 saddle of a young hare, jointed
$\frac{1}{2}$ oz seasoned flour
3 oz butter
1 tablespoon chopped fresh, or $\frac{1}{2}$ teaspoon dried mixed herbs
5 fl oz full-bodied red wine
6 tablespoons Madeira
6 oz button mushrooms

Coat the hare joints in seasoned flour. Melt half the butter in a frying pan and use to brown the joints on all sides. Remove from the pan and place in an ovenproof casserole with the herbs, wine and Madeira. Cover and place in a moderately hot oven (375°C, 190°C, Gas Mark 5) for about 1 hour. Meanwhile, heat the remaining butter and use to sauté the mushrooms for 2 minutes. Add these to the casserole for the last 15 minutes of cooking time.

Liver with sage cream sauce

1 medium onion
1½ oz butter
1 lb lambs' liver
1 tablespoon flour
4 oz mushrooms
1 tablespoon tomato purée
3 tablespoons white wine
1 tablespoon chopped sage
salt and freshly ground black pepper
5 fl oz single cream
2 teaspoons chopped parsley to garnish

Finely chop the onion. Melt 1 oz butter in a large frying pan and use to cook the onion gently for 5 minutes. Slice the liver and coat lightly in the flour. Add remaining butter to the pan and when melted add the liver slices and cook gently for a minute on each side. Slice the mushrooms thinly and add to the pan with the tomato purée and wine. Bring to the boil then reduce heat, add sage and seasoning and stir well. Simmer very gently for 10 minutes, turning the liver once. Remove liver to a heated serving dish, add the cream to the pan, stir well and reheat very gently, stirring constantly. Pour over the liver and sprinkle with parsley before serving.

Kidneys in red wine

4 oz mushrooms
12 lambs' kidneys
1 tablespoon well seasoned flour
2 oz butter
1 large onion, sliced
1 large carrot, sliced
1 tablespoon tomato purée
10 fl oz robust red wine
1 beef stock cube
1 bouquet garni
2 tablespoons hot fried breadcrumbs to garnish

Remove stalks from mushrooms and chop the stalks. Skin, halve and core the kidneys and turn in the seasoned flour. Melt 1½ oz of the butter in a frying pan and use to sauté the kidneys lightly until browned. Remove kidneys to a flame-proof casserole. Add the onion and carrot to the pan and fry lightly. Stir in the remaining flour, tomato purée and wine. Bring to the boil, stirring vigorously, and pour into the casserole. Crumble in the beef stock cube, add the bouquet garni, mushroom stalks and just enough boiling water to cover. Stir well, bring back to boiling point, cover and simmer for about 30 minutes, until the kidneys are tender. Melt remaining butter, and use to sauté the mushroom caps. Remove bouquet garni, and serve the kidneys garnished with mushroom 'cups' filled with hot fried breadcrumbs.

Delicate variety meats, to give a nicer name to offal, go well with mushrooms in white wine sauce. Stronger ones suit red wine sauces with garlic, black olives.

Tripe in white wine

1 knuckle of veal
1 lb tripe
1 oz butter
2 rashers lean bacon
1 clove garlic, crushed
1 large onion, sliced
3 carrots, quartered
dry white wine (see below)
salt and white pepper to taste

Have the knuckle split in half by the butcher. Put it in a saucepan with the tripe, cover with cold water and bring to the boil. Drain. Cut tripe into squares. Melt the butter and use to fry the bacon, garlic, onion and carrot until golden. Put the tripe and knuckle on top and add sufficient wine to cover. Bring to the boil, cover and simmer gently for 3 to 4 hours. Season to taste and serve with boiled potatoes. Serve grated parmesan and paprika in side dishes.

Sweetbreads in cream

1 lb lambs' sweetbreads
2 tablespoons lemon juice
1½ oz butter
4 oz button mushrooms, sliced
1 oz flour
5 fl oz milk
2 tablespoons brandy
1 oz blanched almonds
1 tablespoon chopped parsley
5 fl oz single cream
salt and freshly ground white pepper
2 tablespoons dry white breadcrumbs

Place the sweetbreads in a saucepan, cover with cold water and allow to soak for at least 3 to 4 hours. Add the lemon juice to the pan and bring to the boil. Cover and cook for 5 minutes. Remove sweetbreads and place in cold water. Boil cooking liquid until reduced to 10 fl oz. When sweetbreads are firm, dice, removing any membranes. Heat 1 oz butter in a saucepan and use to fry the mushrooms for about 2 minutes. Stir in the flour until well blended then gradually add the milk, then the meat stock and bring to the boil, stirring constantly, until smooth. Add the brandy, sweetbreads, almonds and parsley. Bring to the boil, remove from the heat and stir in the cream. Add seasoning. Place mixture in an ovenproof dish and stand in a roasting tin of hot water. Melt the remaining butter and use to fry the breadcrumbs until golden. Sprinkle over the sweetbread mixture and cook in a moderate oven (350°F, 180°C, Gas Mark 4) for 30 minutes.

Polder pie

2 oz butter
1 large onion, chopped
1 clove garlic, crushed
1 lb minced beef
1 teaspoon dried basil
1 oz flour
5 fl oz red wine
salt and freshly ground black pepper to taste
12 oz tomatoes, sliced
1 lb creamed potato, hot
3 oz Edam cheese, grated

Melt half the butter and use to sauté the onion and garlic until soft. Add the beef and stir over heat until it changes colour. Add the basil, flour and wine and stir continuously until thick. Reduce heat and cook for a further 10 minutes, stirring frequently. Add seasoning to taste and pour the mixture into a round ovenproof dish. Place two overlapping circles of sliced tomatoes round the dish. Beat up the potato and add 2 oz of the grated

cheese. Pipe potato mixture round edge of dish, put remaining grated cheese in the centre and place in a moderately hot oven (400°F, 200°C, Gas Mark 6) for 25–30 minutes.

Sherried kidneys in rice ring

12 oz lamb's kidneys
1 large onion
2 oz butter
1 clove garlic, crushed
¾ oz flour
1 beef stock cube
9 fl oz water
5 fl oz dry sherry
¼ teaspoon ground bay leaves
salt and freshly ground black pepper to taste
2 packets frozen savoury rice (pimiento and corn)
parsley sprigs to garnish

Remove skins from kidneys, quarter and remove cores. Finely chop the onion. Melt half the butter and use to fry the onion and garlic until soft but not coloured. Add the prepared kidneys and cook very gently for about 3 minutes, stirring frequently, until they have just turned colour. Drain, remove onion and kidneys from the pan and keep hot. Add the remaining butter to the juices in the pan and stir in the flour. Gradually add the stock cube dissolved in the water and the sherry. Bring to the boil, stirring constantly, until sauce is thick and smooth. Replace the kidneys and onion and add the ground bay leaves and seasoning. Bring back to the boil and simmer gently, uncovered, for 5 minutes, until kidneys are just cooked. Adjust seasoning. Meanwhile, cook the rice according to directions on the packet. Drain and press into a greased ring mould. Turn out on to a hot serving dish and spoon the kidneys and

sauce into the centre. Garnish with parsley sprigs.
Note: If you prefer to use 3 packets frozen braised kidneys in gravy, reduce the sherry by half and stir in just before serving.

Jambalaya

1 mild onion
1 sweet pepper
2 oz butter
1 tablespoon oil
1 clove garlic, crushed
6 oz cooked ham, diced
6 oz prawns, shelled
4 oz chorizo or other boiling sausage, sliced
5 fl oz dry white wine
15 oz can tomatoes
¼ teaspoon dried oregano
½ teaspoon dried basil
¼ teaspoon Tabasco
salt and freshly ground black pepper
8 oz long grain rice

Finely chop the onion, deseed and finely chop the pepper. Heat the butter and oil together in a flameproof casserole and use to sauté the onion, pepper and garlic until limp. Stir in the ham, prawns and sausage and cook for a minute. Add the wine, tomatoes, herbs, Tabasco and seasoning and bring to the boil. Add the rice, cover and simmer until rice is tender. This takes from 30 to 40 minutes, according to the kind of rice.

Réchauffé fin

1 cooked calves' tongue (about 1½ lbs)
8 oz cooked white meat (veal, chicken, pork)
5 oz butter
1½ oz seasoned flour
15 fl oz chicken stock
4 oz mushrooms
2 oz can anchovy fillets, drained
1 tablespoon capers, drained

2 tablespoons chopped gherkin
6 tablespoons dry white wine
2 egg yolks, beaten
2 tablespoons dry white breadcrumbs
lemon slices to garnish

Cut all the meats into small dice. Melt 4 oz butter, stir in the flour and cook until golden. Add the stock gradually and bring to the boil, stirring constantly. Chop the mushrooms finely and add to the sauce, bring back to boiling point and simmer for 10 minutes. Reserve six anchovy fillets and chop the rest. Add these to the sauce with the capers, gherkin, and the wine. Put in the meat and stir well. Remove from heat and add the beaten egg yolks. Pack the mixture into six buttered ramekin dishes and place a halved anchovy fillet crisscross over the top of each. Sprinkle with breadcrumbs and dot with the remaining butter. Place in a hot oven (425°F, 220°C, Gas Mark 7) for 10 to 12 minutes. Serve garnished with lemon slices. (Serves 6.)

My moussaka

3 oz butter
8 oz onions, chopped
12 oz minced cooked lamb
4 tablespoons chopped parsley
8 oz tomatoes, chopped
salt and freshly ground black pepper
5 fl oz stock or thin gravy
1½ lbs potatoes, sliced
4 tablespoons red wine
2 tablespoons flour
10 fl oz milk
1 egg, beaten
1 oz cheese, grated

Melt 2½ oz butter and use to fry the onions gently until softened. Add the meat, parsley and tomatoes and cook gently for 2 minutes. Season well and moisten with the stock. Place a thin layer of potato slices in a greased ovenproof dish and cover with a layer of meat. Repeat the layers, finishing with one of potatoes. Sprinkle with the wine. Melt the remaining butter in a small saucepan, add the flour and cook for 1 minute. Add the milk gradually and bring to the boil, stirring constantly, until smooth and thickened. Remove from heat and stir in the egg and the cheese. Pour over the potatoes and bake in a moderate oven (350°F, 180°C, Gas Mark 4) for an hour. Serve cut into wedges.

Casseroles

Removing the lid from a casserole dish cooked with wine is one of life's great joys. The rich aroma of mingled flavours is tempting to the appetite and balm to the soul. Enjoy it more often.

Italian lamb stew

3 lbs boned shoulder of lamb
salt and freshly ground black pepper
6 tablespoons oil
4 oz butter
2 large onions, sliced
10 fl oz dry white wine
1 teaspoon dried basil
15 oz can tomatoes
2 oz mushrooms
15 oz can butter beans, drained

Cut the meat into neat cubes and season with salt and pepper. Heat the oil and 2 oz butter in a flameproof casserole and use to cook the onions until soft but not coloured. Add the meat and seal on all sides. Pour in the wine and simmer gently for about 20 minutes until the moisture has almost evaporated. Pour in the chopped tomatoes and juice from the can and the herbs. Cover and place in a moderately hot oven (375°F, 190°C, Gas Mark 5) for about 1½ hours, or until the meat is tender. Add the mushrooms and beans for the last 30 minutes.

Porc à la fermière

4 large pork chops, or thick slices belly pork
2 pigs' kidneys
1 cooking apple
1 teaspoon dried sage
1 large onion, sliced
salt and freshly ground black pepper
1½ teaspoons soft brown sugar
1 tablespoon tomato purée
1½ lbs potatoes, sliced
10 tablespoons red wine

Remove skin from pork chops. Skin the kidneys, remove cores and cut into slices. Peel the apple and cut into thin slices. Arrange the pieces of pork and slices of kidney in layers in an ovenproof casserole, alternating with layers of apple, sage, onion, seasoning, sugar and tomato purée. Cover with a thick layer of potatoes. Pour over the wine, cover and cook in a cool oven (300°F, 150°C, Gas Mark 2) for 3 hours. If necessary add a little water towards the end of cooking time.

Soak a whole pound of haricot beans overnight; just 4 oz is sufficient when cooked and drained to mix with chopped spring onions, parsley and wine vinaigrette to serve as a cold Provençale salad.

Osso buco

2 veal hocks
2 tablespoons flour
1 oz butter
1 large carrot, chopped
2 onions, chopped
10 fl oz white wine
2 tablespoons tomato purée
½ teaspoon dried rosemary
1 teaspoon salt
¼ teaspoon freshly ground white pepper
1 chicken stock cube
10 fl oz boiling water
1 teaspoon finely grated lemon zest and 1 tablespoon chopped parsley to garnish.

Have the butcher chop the veal into 2 inch cubes. Coat the veal in the flour. Melt the butter in a large flameproof casserole and use to fry the meat, carrot and onion in it until well browned. Add the wine, tomato purée, rosemary and seasoning. Make up the stock cube with the boiling water and add to the casserole with more water if necessary to cover the meat. Bring to the boil, cover and simmer for 1 to 1½ hours, or until tender. Sprinkle with the lemon zest and chopped parsley.

Haricot pork casserole

12 oz haricot beans
2 tablespoons flour
2 teaspoons salt
½ teaspoon chilli powder
¼ teaspoon freshly ground black pepper
4 lbs bladebone of pork, cubed
2 tablespoons oil
1 lb 13-oz can tomatoes
20 fl oz dry red wine
2 bay leaves
4 carrots, sliced
8 baby onions, sliced
3 sticks celery, sliced

Wine-glazed Chicken

Soak the beans in cold water overnight. Season the flour with the salt, chilli powder and pepper and use to coat the meat. Heat the oil in a flameproof casserole, add the meat and cook quickly until browned on all sides. Drain off excess oil. Add the drained soaked beans, tomatoes, wine and bay leaves. Bring to the boil, cover and simmer for 1¼ hours. Add the vegetables and cook for a further 20 minutes.

Transylvanian goulash

1½ lbs boned pork, diced
4 medium onions, chopped
1 clove garlic, crushed
1 teaspoon caraway seeds
1 teaspoon salt
1 beef stock cube
10 fl oz boiling water
10 fl oz dry white wine
15 oz can sauerkraut
4 teaspoons paprika
10 fl oz soured cream

Trim fat from meat and render it slowly in a large flameproof casserole. When the pan is well greased, put in the meat, onions, garlic, caraway seeds and salt and stir well. Make up the stock cube with the boiling water and pour over the meat with the wine. Bring to the boil, cover and simmer for an hour. Add the sauerkraut and liquid from the can and the paprika dissolved in a little of the hot liquid from the casserole. Return to the boil, cover and simmer for a further 45 minutes, or until the meat is tender. Remove from heat and stir in the cream. Serve with plain boiled potatoes turned in melted butter and sprinkled with chopped parsley.

Cossetted gammon

3 lb joint of gammon
1½ oz butter
8 oz button onions
8 oz small carrots
15 oz can tomatoes
5 fl oz dry white wine
1 teaspoon dried oregano
freshly ground white pepper
2 tablespoons dry white breadcrumbs

Soak the joint in cold water for 12 hours, or overnight if possible. Drain and place in a saucepan. Cover with fresh water, bring to the boil, cover and simmer for 50 minutes. Drain off liquid, remove rind from the gammon and discard. Place the joint in a large ovenproof casserole. Melt 1 oz of the butter in another pan and use to fry the onions and carrots until golden, pour off excess fat and add the tomatoes, wine, herbs and pepper to taste. Bring to the boil and pour round the joint. Cover and cook in a moderately hot oven (375°F, 190°C, Gas Mark 5) for an hour. Meanwhile, melt remaining butter, add breadcrumbs and stir over moderate heat until golden brown. Sprinkle joint with crumbs and serve surrounded by the vegetables.

Braised chicken with apricots

8 oz dried apricots
2 carrots, sliced
1 large onion, sliced
bouquet garni
1 boiling chicken (about 4 lbs)
5 fl oz dry white wine
salt and freshly ground white pepper

Put the apricots, carrots, onion and bouquet garni into the bottom of a large

Sherried Kidneys in Rice Ring

deep casserole. Place the chicken on top, pour over the wine and sprinkle with salt and pepper. Bring to the boil, cover tightly and simmer for an hour. Meanwhile cook the giblets in 10 fl oz water. Strain giblet stock into the braise, remove bouquet garni and serve with buttered rice. (Serves 6.)

Coq au vin rouge

1 chicken (about 3 lbs), jointed
2 tablespoons seasoned flour
2 oz butter
1 tablespoon oil
1 large onion, chopped
4 tablespoons brandy or marc
10 fl oz full-bodied red wine
salt and freshly ground black pepper
2 cloves garlic, crushed
4 oz smoked fat bacon, diced
12 button onions
4 oz button mushrooms, sliced

Coat the chicken portions in seasoned flour. Heat the butter and oil together in a flameproof casserole and use to fry the chopped onion until softened. Add the chicken portions and cook until golden brown on all sides. Warm the brandy in a ladle or small pan, ignite and pour over the chicken. When the flames die down add the wine, seasoning and garlic. Bring to the boil, cover and simmer for about an hour, until really tender. Fry bacon in a clean pan until the fat runs freely. Remove bacon and use fat to fry the button onions for 3 minutes. Put in the mushrooms and sauté lightly. Add onions and mushrooms to the casserole and simmer for a further 20 minutes. The sauce can be further thickened with beurre manié if desired.

Chicken in sour cream

1 oz butter
1 large onion, chopped
4 oz lean bacon
2 small roasting chickens
salt and freshly ground white pepper
1 chicken stock cube
15 fl oz boiling water
2 bay leaves
5 fl oz red wine
$\frac{1}{2}$ lemon
sauce :
1 oz butter
1 oz flour
4 oz mushrooms
5 fl oz soured cream

Melt the butter and use to sauté the onion gently for 2 minutes. Derind and chop the bacon, add to the pan and fry until the fat begins to run. Transfer to an ovenproof casserole deep enough to take the chickens easily, and place the birds on top. Season lightly with salt and pepper. Make up the stock cube with the boiling water and pour round the birds. Add the bay leaves, wine, the juice of the lemon and the squeezed half of lemon. Bring to the boil, cover and place in a moderate oven (350°F, 180°C, Gas Mark 4) for about an hour, until tender. Remove chickens from casserole and strain the stock. Replace chickens. To make the sour cream sauce, melt the butter and stir in the flour. Add the strained stock gradually and bring to the boil, stirring constantly until smooth and thick. Add the mushrooms and simmer for 5 minutes. Remove from the heat, add the soured cream and stir until well blended. Adjust seasoning and pour sauce over the chickens. (Serves 6.)

Note : I use a covered dimpled roasting tin.

Poularde braisée au porto

1 chicken (3 to 4 lbs)
8 oz button mushrooms
4 oz goose liver pâté
salt and freshly ground white pepper
3 oz butter
1 onion, chopped
1 carrot, chopped
1 bacon rasher, diced
bouquet garni
4 tablespoons port
parsley sprigs to garnish

Stuff the chicken with half the mushrooms and the pâté, and sprinkle with salt and pepper. Melt the butter in a flameproof casserole and use to fry the onion, carrot, remaining mushrooms and bacon until onion is slightly softened. Add the bouquet garni and place the chicken on top. Pour over the port and sufficient water just to come through the vegetables. Cook uncovered in a moderately hot oven (375°F, 190°C, Gas Mark 5) for 15 minutes, then reduce heat to moderate (350°F, 180°C, Gas Mark 4) cover and braise for a further 1½ hours. Place chicken on a heated serving dish, remove bouquet garni, liquidize or sieve the vegetables and juices and adjust seasoning. Garnish chicken with parsley and serve the sauce separately.

Estouffade of chicken

1 oz flour
salt and freshly ground white pepper
1 roasting chicken, jointed
1 oz lard
2 large onions, chopped
8 oz mushrooms, chopped
1 teaspoon dried rosemary
1 chicken stock cube

15 fl oz boiling water
5 fl oz dry white wine

Season the flour well and use to coat the chicken portions. Melt the lard and fry the chicken in it until golden brown on all sides. Remove to an ovenproof casserole. Add the onion to the pan and fry until slightly softened, then add this to the chicken. Put the mushrooms into the remaining fat and sauté lightly. Add to the chicken with the rosemary. Make up the stock cube with the boiling water and add to the casserole with the wine. Crinkle a long strip of kitchen foil, about 3 inches wide and long enough to go round the dish. Press it well to the top edge of the casserole and push the lid into place to seal it completely. Cook in the lower part of a cool oven (275°F, 140°C, Gas Mark 1) for 3 to 4 hours.

Duck with red cabbage

1 lb red cabbage, shredded
4 duck portions
1 tablespoon oil
½ teaspoon salt
5 fl oz red wine
5 fl oz soured cream

Blanch the cabbage in boiling water for 2 minutes, then drain. Brush the duck portions with oil and sprinkle with salt. Heat the remaining oil in a frying pan and use to brown the duck portions quickly on all sides. Arrange a layer of red cabbage in an ovenproof casserole, lay the duck portions on this and cover with the remaining cabbage. Mix together the wine and soured cream and pour over the casserole. Cover and cook in a moderately hot oven (375°F, 190°C, Gas Mark 5) for 1 to 1½ hours until the duck is tender.

Pigeon casserole with chestnuts

8 oz chestnuts
1 oz butter
2 tablespoons oil
2 plump pigeons, split
4 small onions, sliced
2 tablespoons flour
5 fl oz rosé wine
1 beef stock cube
10 fl oz boiling water
1 orange
1 teaspoon cranberry jelly
$\frac{1}{4}$ teaspoon salt
pinch freshly ground black pepper
bouquet garni

Simmer, drain, split and skin the chestnuts. Heat together the butter and oil and use to brown the pigeon halves, remove and transfer to an ovenproof casserole. Add the onion to the pan, fry until slightly softened, drain and put this with the pigeon halves. Brown the chestnuts in the remaining oil, remove and reserve. Stir flour into the juices in the pan and cook until brown. Gradually stir in the wine and stock cube made up with the boiling water. Bring to the boil, stirring constantly, and pour into the casserole. Cut off a thick piece of rind from the orange and squeeze the juice. Add these to the casserole with the cranberry jelly, seasoning and bouquet garni. Cover and place in a moderate oven (325°F, 170°C, Gas Mark 3) for 1$\frac{1}{2}$ hours. Add the chestnuts for the last 40 minutes of cooking time. Remove orange rind and bouquet garni before serving.

Note: Canned whole chestnuts can be used but add these to the casserole for the last 20 minutes of cooking time only, or they will disintegrate.

Hare with prunes and chestnuts

8 oz prunes
$\frac{1}{2}$ pint hot tea, strained
1 young hare, jointed
1 bottle dry white wine
1 carrot, sliced
1 onion, sliced
salt and freshly ground white pepper
$\frac{1}{2}$ teaspoon dried rosemary
$\frac{1}{2}$ teaspoon dried thyme
2 oz seasoned flour
2 tablespoons oil
4 tablespoons brandy
8 button onions
4 oz lean bacon, diced
1 lb chestnuts
fried bread croûtons to garnish

Put the prunes in a basin, pour over the hot tea and leave to soak for 24 hours. Place the hare pieces in a shallow dish. Mix together the wine, sliced carrot, onion, seasoning and herbs and pour over the hare. Allow to stand for 24 hours, turning occasionally. Drain hare pieces and dry on absorbent kitchen paper. Coat in seasoned flour. Heat the oil in a flameproof casserole and use to brown the hare pieces on all sides. Warm the brandy in a ladle or small pan, ignite and pour over the meat. When flames die down, strain over the remaining marinade, and sufficient water just to cover the meat. Add the button onions, bacon and seasoning. Bring to the boil, cover and simmer for an hour. Boil the chestnuts, peel and add to the casserole. Cook for a further 2 hours. 10 minutes before end of cooking time, drain the prunes, stone them and add to the casserole with the gently fried and sieved liver of the hare. Stir well. If the blood from the hare is available, gently heat and stir into the sauce.

Salmis of game

2 oz butter
1 guinea fowl or partridge, or 2 pigeons
salt and freshly ground black pepper
10 fl oz water
2 oz fat bacon
1 clove garlic, crushed
1 tablespoon silverskin pickled onions
4 oz chopped onion
4 oz chopped carrot
2 tablespoons brandy
$\frac{1}{2}$ bottle dry red wine
grated nutmeg
bouquet garni
$\frac{3}{4}$ oz butter
$\frac{1}{2}$ oz flour

Melt the butter in a flameproof casserole and use to brown the game, season with salt and pepper and cover. Cook over a low heat for 30 minutes. Remove the bird or birds from the casserole and carve into serving pieces. Keep hot. Cut the carcase, wings and giblets into pieces and place in a saucepan with the water. Bring to the boil, cover and simmer for 20 minutes. Cut bacon into snippets and cook gently in the casserole together with the garlic, pickled onions and chopped vegetables for 5 minutes. Warm the brandy in a ladle or small pan, ignite and pour into the casserole. Add the wine and just sufficient of the strained giblet stock to cover the contents. Season with more pepper and grated nutmeg, add the bouquet garni, cover and simmer for 45 minutes. Remove bouquet garni. Knead together the butter and flour to make beurre manié and add this to the casserole in small pieces, stir in the game pieces and reheat.

Note: This dish can be garnished with crescent shaped fried bread croûtons.

Casserole de faisan

1 plump pheasant
salt and freshly ground black pepper
3 oz butter
4 oz button mushrooms, quartered
6 tablespoons Calvados or brandy
$\frac{1}{4}$ fresh root of horseradish, grated, or 2 tablespoons creamed horseradish
5 fl oz veal or chicken stock
10 fl oz double cream

Cut the pheasant into quarters and remove breast bones. Sprinkle with salt and pepper. Put the pheasant into an ovenproof casserole with the butter and place uncovered in a hot oven (425°F, 220°C, Gas Mark 7) for 5 minutes. Turn the pieces and replace in oven for a further 5 minutes. Lower oven heat to moderate (350°F, 180°C, Gas Mark 4), add mushrooms to the casserole, cover and return to the oven for 10 minutes. Warm the Calvados or brandy in a ladle or small pan, ignite and pour over the pheasant. Mix together the horseradish and stock and when the flames have died down, pour over the casserole. Cover and return to the oven for a further 15 minutes. Turn off the oven, take out the casserole, pour the cream over and leave in the oven for a few minutes before serving.

Garenne à l'Alsacienne

1 young rabbit
8 oz streaky bacon
5 fl oz white wine
salt and freshly ground black pepper
2 lb red cabbage, shredded
10 juniper berries
4 tablespoons brandy

Joint the rabbit. Derind the bacon and fry in a large flameproof casserole until the fat begins to run, then put in the rabbit joints and brown them on all sides. Pour in the wine and seasoning. Bring to the boil, cover and reduce the heat to simmer. Meanwhile, in another pan, boil the cabbage in salted water for 5 minutes, then drain. Place in the casserole with the rabbit, cover and simmer for an hour. Add the juniper berries and cook for a further 10 minutes. Warm the brandy in a ladle or small pan, ignite and pour over the casserole. When the flames have died down, cook for a further 5 minutes.

Dishes from the freezer

Long ago, I decided to stop paying the earth for so-called gourmet dishes from a freezer centre when I could produce my own at half the price. So can you.

Freezing meat casseroles

As the cooking instructions are for large quantities, it may be necessary to divide the ingredients between two casseroles. All meat casseroles should be cooled, packed with 1 inch headspace, and sealed for freezing.

In the former case, if two portions for six people suit your family requirements, you may decide to freeze the food in the casseroles in which it has been cooked. I can usually spare one for a short time but prefer to pack two smaller portions separately in rigid-based polythene containers with snap-on seals. These can be placed under hot water to loosen the contents which then turn out easily into a saucepan for reheating. Alternatively, if you pack in shaped foil containers, these can go straight into the oven from the freezer, standing them on a baking sheet as the contents sometimes bubble out.

Defrosting and reheating safely

If time permits, defrost fully, still covered, in the original container in the refrigerator overnight, or up to 24 hours for a really large one. Small portions of course take relatively less time to defrost. This ensures that the cooked food reheats evenly and that you are not left with any pockets of frozen resistance. If speed is essential and the container will not stand oven heat, you must loosen the contents and turn them into a heavy based saucepan. Reheating is aided by the addition of a little liquid (water or extra stock for instance) as this prevents the food from sticking and burning while most of it is still in the frozen state. Break up gently with a fork every few minutes until even defrosting and reheating has been achieved. If the container is ovenproof, put it into a moderately hot oven (400°F, 200°C, Gas Mark 6) allowing rather less than an hour for containers holding up to 40 fl oz and rather more than an hour for larger ones. After the first 30 minutes, you should try to stir and break up the contents lightly.

Veal marengo

4 lbs boned shoulder of veal, cubed
4 tablespoons seasoned flour
6 tablespoons oil
4 onions, chopped
2 cloves garlic, crushed
4 tablespoons tomato purée
15 fl oz dry white wine
10 fl oz chicken stock

½ teaspoon dried marjoram
4 bay leaves
salt and freshly ground white pepper
24 button mushrooms

Toss the veal in the seasoned flour. Heat the oil in a flameproof casserole and use to fry the onion and garlic until soft but not coloured. Add the veal cubes and fry until golden on all sides. Stir in the tomato purée, wine and stock and bring to the boil, stirring constantly. Add the herbs and seasoning, cover and simmer for 1 hour. Add the mushrooms and continue cooking for a further 30 minutes.

Vintners' veal casserole

4 lbs boned shoulder of veal
10 fl oz white wine
4 tablespoons oil
2 strips lemon rind
2 strips orange rind
2 sprigs thyme (lemon thyme, if possible)
2 large onions
2 large cloves garlic, optional
salt and freshly ground white pepper
1 lb sweet green peppers
1 lb 13 oz can tomatoes
1 lb courgettes
3 tablespoons cornflour

Cut the meat into large cubes and place in a shallow dish with the wine, oil, fruit rinds and herbs. Slice the onion and finely chop the garlic and add to the marinade with salt and pepper. Leave to stand for at least 2 hours, turning occasionally. Deseed the peppers, slice thinly and blanch the slices in boiling water for a minute. Drain. Place the veal, marinade and blanched pepper together in an ovenproof casserole and add the tomatoes. Cover and cook in a cool oven (275°F, 140°C, Gas Mark 1) for about 2 hours. Meanwhile, cut the courgettes into ½ inch slices, blanch in boiling water for a minute and add to the casserole. Moisten the cornflour with a little cold water, add to the casserole and stir well. Adjust seasoning and return to the oven for a further 30 minutes, until veal is tender and the courgettes cooked.

Marinaded beef

5 lbs braising steak, cubed
10 fl oz red wine
4 tablespoons oil
1 tablespoon dried oregano
2 cloves garlic, crushed
salt and freshly ground black pepper
1 large onion
8 oz salt belly of pork or streaky bacon
20 fl oz beef stock
4 teaspoons cornflour

Place the beef in a shallow dish with the wine, half the oil and the oregano. Add garlic to the marinade with the salt and pepper. Allow to stand for at least 2 hours, turning occasionally. Chop the onion finely. Derind and chop the pork or bacon. Heat the oil in a frying pan and use to sauté the onion and bacon for about 5 minutes. Drain the pieces of beef, place in the pan and seal on all sides over high heat. Remove beef, onion and bacon to a large ovenproof casserole and pour over the marinade. Pour stock into frying pan and stir well, scraping up any juices from the meat. Pour over the casserole. Cover and cook in a moderate oven (325°F, 170°C, Gas Mark 3) for 1½ to 2 hours, until the beef is tender. Moisten the cornflour with 2 tablespoons water, stir into the juices in the casserole and return to the oven for a further 15 minutes.

Sherried kidneys

5 fl oz olive oil
3 large onions, chopped
3 cloves garlic, crushed
3 bay leaves
6 tablespoons flour
1½ beef stock cubes
15 fl oz boiling water
4 oz chopped parsley
3 lbs lambs' kidneys
salt and freshly ground black pepper
scant 10 fl oz dry sherry

Heat half the oil in a saucepan and use to cook the onion, garlic and bay leaves for about 5 minutes, until onion is soft but not coloured. Add the flour and stir until well blended. Make up the stock cubes with the boiling water and add gradually to the pan. Bring to the boil, stirring constantly. Add the parsley to the pan and simmer for 5 minutes. Remove bay leaves. Wash the kidneys, cut in half and remove skins and cores. Season well. Heat the remaining oil in a frying pan and use to cook the kidneys quickly, stirring over high heat for 7 to 8 minutes. Remove kidneys and pour sherry into the juices in the pan. Replace kidneys, onion mixture. Stir well and reheat.

Sportsman's pâté

1 lb streaky bacon, diced
3 lbs pigs' liver, sliced
3 large onions, chopped
6 cloves garlic, crushed
1 teaspoon dried marjoram
½ teaspoon ground allspice
4 juniper berries
salt and freshly ground black pepper
1 bottle dry red wine
12 oz butter

Place the bacon, liver, onion, garlic, herbs, spices and seasoning and wine in a large boiling basin. Stir and then press ingredients down so that they are covered by the wine. Cover the basin and steam for 4 hours. Cool slightly. Strain off the liquid and reserve. Liquidize the mixture in a blender and add sufficient reserved liquid to make a thick paste. Keep surplus liquid for following recipe. Melt the butter, add to the meat mixture and liquidize again.

To freeze: Pack while still warm into three 1 lb loaf tins or polythene containers. Cool. Cover loaf tins with foil and smooth down edges or snap seal on containers. Label and date each container.

To serve: Take from freezer and defrost at room temperature for about 4 hours.

Sportsman's stew

2½ lbs lean stewing beef, diced
2 tablespoons seasoned flour
1 oz lard
1 tablespoon olive oil
8 oz fat salt pork, diced
1 onion, sliced
5 fl oz reserved liquid (see Sportsman's pâté)
2 tablespoons orange juice
1 teaspoon grated orange zest
4 tablespoons tomato purée
salt and freshly ground black pepper

Turn the beef in the seasoned flour. Heat the lard and oil in a flameproof casserole and use to sauté the pork and onion until golden. Add the beef and cook quickly until browned on all sides. Stir in the reserved liquid, orange juice and zest, the tomato purée and enough water to cover the meat barely. Bring to the boil, cover and simmer for 2 hours, or until meat is tender. Adjust seasoning if necessary.

Pain de foie aux herbes

1½ lbs chicken livers
3 medium onions, chopped
3 cloves garlic, crushed
1 lb sausagemeat
3 eggs, beaten
salt and freshly ground black pepper
¼ teaspoon dried thyme
¼ teaspoon dried marjoram
3 tablespoons brandy
6 tablespoons sherry
12 rashers streaky bacon
6 bay leaves

Cut the livers up roughly and liquidize them in a blender with the onion and garlic. Turn into a basin and mix with the sausagemeat, eggs, seasoning, herbs, brandy and sherry. Divide the mixture between three 20 fl oz terrines or 1 lb loaf tins. Derind the bacon, arrange four rashers on each container, and place the bay leaves on top. Put the containers in a large roasting tin, pour boiling water round them to come half-way up and cook in a hot oven (425°F, 220°C, Gas Mark 7) for 45 minutes. Cool.

To freeze: Cover the containers with freezer foil and smooth down the edges. Label and date.

To serve: Allow to defrost at room temperature for about 4 hours.

Never throw away precious cooking aids such as the reserved liquid mentioned left. If not using at once, refrigerate up to 4 days and add to any red meat stew, or freeze in small containers for future use.

Halibut in white wine sauce

4 halibut steaks
2 onions, sliced
20 fl oz dry white wine
1 teaspoon dried tarragon
2 bay leaves
4 oz butter
4 oz button mushrooms, sliced
1 oz flour
salt and freshly ground black pepper
to serve:
1 oz butter
4 oz shelled prawns
16 Spanish stuffed green olives, sliced
few prawns in the shell to garnish

Place fish steaks, a few slices of onion, wine, tarragon and bay leaves in an oven-proof dish, cover and cook in a moderate oven (350°F, 170°C, Gas Mark 3) for 20 minutes, or until fish is cooked. Lift out fish and drain. Meanwhile, melt 4 oz butter and use to fry the remaining onion and the mushrooms for 3 minutes. Strain the cooking liquid from fish and reserve. Remove bay leaf, add onion and mushroom to fish. Add flour to melted butter in pan and cook without browning. Gradually add the liquid from the fish, stirring constantly. Bring to the boil and cook for one minute. Cool.

To freeze: Place fish in a shaped foil container with sauce. Seal, label and date.

To serve: Place container in a moderate oven (350°F, 180°C, Gas Mark 4) for about 45 minutes. Remove fish to a heated serving dish. Meanwhile, melt 1 oz butter, lightly sauté prawns and olives. Stir in the fish sauce. Beat together 2 egg yolks and 2 tablespoons cream, add to the sauce and reheat without boiling. Pour over the fish, garnish with prawns in the shell.

Spanish chicken with olives

1 chicken (3½ to 4 lbs), jointed
2 tablespoons oil
1 oz butter
1 large onion, chopped
2 oz mushrooms, sliced
1 green pepper
4 streaky bacon rashers, chopped
1 clove garlic, crushed
1 tablespoon flour
5 fl oz chicken stock
10 fl oz Spanish red burgundy
bouquet garni
¼ teaspoon marjoram
salt and freshly ground black pepper
gravy browning
10 Spanish stuffed green olives
2 tablespoons brandy

Heat oil and butter in a frying pan. Add the chicken joints and cook until golden brown. Remove chicken from pan, take off the skin if preferred, then put in an ovenproof casserole. Put onion, mushrooms and deseeded and sliced green pepper into the frying pan with the bacon and garlic and cook until soft. Remove and add to chicken. Stir flour into fat remaining in frying pan and cook until butter is just turning brown. Gradually add stock, stirring all the time. Add the wine and pour over the chicken and vegetables. Add bouquet garni, marjoram, salt and pepper and stir well. Cook in a moderate oven (350°F, 180°C, Gas Mark 4) for about 45 minutes, or until the chicken is cooked. Check seasoning and add gravy browning if necessary. Stir in olives and brandy. Cool.

To freeze: Divide between 2 polythene containers. Seal, label and date.

To serve: Defrost completely, turn into a heavy based saucepan and reheat to boiling point. Simmer for 5 minutes, stirring frequently.

Lamb cutlets en croûte

12 lamb cutlets
1 oz butter
2 tablespoons oil
2 lbs puff pastry
2 eggs, beaten
mushroom filling:
4 oz long grain rice
2 oz butter
8 oz mushrooms, finely sliced
salt and freshly ground black pepper to taste
6 tablespoons red wine

To make the mushroom filling, cook the long grain rice in salted water until tender, drain and cool. Sauté the mushrooms in the butter, mix with the rice, season, then add sufficient wine to moisten (about 6 tablespoons). Trim off the meat and scrape bones clean for about an inch on all the cutlets. Heat together the butter and oil and use to brown the cutlets on both sides. Drain and cool. Roll out the pastry thinly and cut into 12 equal squares, each large enough to enclose a cutlet completely. Place a little filling in the centre of each pastry square, top this with a cutlet, season and spoon over any remaining filling. Brush the edges of the pastry with beaten egg and fold each piece to enclose the cutlet closely, sealing the edges well together. Roll out trimmings and cut leaves to decorate. Place on a damped baking sheet, with the join underneath, and brush with beaten egg. Bake in a hot oven (425°F, 220°C, Gas Mark 7) for 25 to 30 minutes, until well risen and golden brown. Cool.

To freeze: Wrap each cutlet individually in foil and pack them together in a large polythene container. Seal, label and date.

To serve: Place still frozen on a baking sheet and reheat in a hot oven (as above) for 20 to 25 minutes. Decorate each protruding bone with a cutlet frill and serve hot.

Moulded brandy syllabubs

4 tablespoons caster sugar
finely grated zest and juice of 1 lemon
2 tablespoons sherry
1 tablespoon brandy
10 fl oz double cream
little whipped cream and glacé cherries to decorate

Dissolve the sugar in the lemon juice, sherry and brandy. Add the lemon zest. Whip the cream until it forms soft peaks then gradually whisk in the lemon mixture.

To freeze: Pour into four rinsed Tupperware Jellettes, seal and label.

To serve: Take from freezer, dip in hot water and turn out onto serving plates. Decorate each one with a rosette of whipped cream and a glacé cherry.

Gaelic syllabub

1½ teaspoons instant coffee powder
3 tablespoons caster sugar
4 tablespoons boiling water
4 tablespoons Irish whiskey
1 teaspoon lemon juice
10 fl oz double cream
glacé cherries to decorate

Dissolve coffee and sugar in boiling water. Add the whiskey and lemon juice. Whip

the cream until it forms soft peaks, then gradually whisk in the coffee mixture. Pour into small polythene containers, cover with foil, seal and freeze.

To serve: Take straight from the freezer, dip in hot water and turn out. Decorate each with a glacé cherry.

Madeira mousse

5 egg yolks
5 tablespoons caster sugar
4 tablespoons Madeira
few drops red food colouring
2 egg whites

Beat the egg yolks, sugar and Madeira together in a double boiler over gently boiling water, until doubled in volume. Add colouring. Fold in the stiffly beaten egg whites just before serving then pour into parfait dishes and either serve warm, or cover with foil, seal, label and freeze.

To serve: Unseal and allow to stand at room temperature for 10 minutes.

Flambé dishes

The reason for igniting a spirit or liqueur is to drive off the alcoholic content and leave only the essence of its flavour. The flames singe the surface of the food slightly, giving an attractive flavour.

Sometimes, for instance if there is surplus fat in the pan, it may flare up alarmingly. On the other hand it is sometimes sulky or refuses to ignite at all. For the amateur, flambé cooking is quite an adventure. Here are some simple rules to ensure success.

1. If difficult to ignite, the spirit is probably too cold, and should be heated

in a small pan or ladle to make the alcohol more volatile. Put a lighted match or taper to it at arm's length, and as soon as it flames, pour it over the food.

2. To make certain that it burns well and for a satisfying length of time, sprinkle a little sugar over the food before it is flambéed. This ensures a reasonably dramatic demonstration but is only recommended for sweet dishes or rich meat dishes where the resulting caramel will enhance the flavour.

3. For the best result, copy the restaurant technique; shake the pan gently over the source of heat and spoon the flaming liquid several times over the food.

Resist the temptation to serve the food the instant the flames have gone out, but continue cooking for a further 2 to 3 minutes so that all traces of the raw flavour of alcohol disappear and the full rounded flavour of the finished sauce develops.

If you have a steady hand, a suitable chafing dish, and sufficient élan to carry it off successfully, flambé cooking at the table in front of your guests is just about the best piece of wineupmanship I know. For those without a chafing dish or with less nerve, the same effect can be achieved by igniting the spirit in the kitchen and bearing the dish, triumphantly aflame, to the table.

Fish flamed with fennel

4 small trout or mackerel, gutted
2 tablespoons olive oil
salt and freshly ground black pepper
4 dried sprigs of fennel
2 tablespoons brandy

Make several slashes on each side of the fish and place them on the grid of a grill pan. Brush with oil and sprinkle with salt

and pepper. Cook under the grill for 4 minutes, turn them over, brush with oil again, season and cook as before. Lift the grid from the pan, leaving the fish in place. Place the fennel sprigs in the grill pan and replace the grid. Warm the brandy in a ladle or small pan, ignite and pour over the fish. The sprigs of herbs will catch alight and the resulting smoke will give a most unusual and subtle flavour to the fish. When the flames die down, replace the fish under the hot grill and cook for a further 3 minutes on each side, or until cooked.

Note: You can buy dried fennel sprigs in boxes of mixed dried *herbes de Provence* in delicatessen shops.

Steak Diane

2 thin slices sirloin steak
freshly ground black pepper
1 button onion or shallot
½ teaspoon Worcestershire sauce
2 tablespoons brandy, warmed
1 tablespoon chopped parsley to garnish

Rub a little pepper into the meat on both sides. Chop the onion very finely. Melt the butter and use to fry the onion until pale golden, little more than a minute. Add the steaks and cook for about 1 minute on each side or a little longer if you want them well done. Remove meat and keep it hot. Add the Worcestershire sauce, stir well to combine with the onion and pan juices. Add the warmed brandy and ignite, return the steaks to the pan and continue cooking for a further minute. Serve garnished with chopped parsley.

Note: This dish can be extended to serve four steaks if the quantity of other ingredients is doubled and four smaller, thicker steaks are chosen so that they will all fit into the pan together.

Pêches flambées

15 fl oz milk
2½ oz caster sugar
2 oz round grain rice
5 fl oz double cream
3 tablespoons Kirsch
1 oz mixed candied fruits, chopped
2 peaches
4 cubes of sugar

Place the milk, sugar and rice in a saucepan and cook very gently, stirring frequently, until the rice is cooked and has absorbed all the liquid. Allow to cool. Whip the cream lightly, fold in 2 tablespoons of the liqueur and then fold the flavoured cream into the cold rice with the candied fruit. Pour into a glass serving dish. Halve the peaches and remove stones. Place the peach halves, cut side up, on top of the rice mixture and press down slightly. Warm the remaining liqueur and soak the cubes of sugar in it. Place one in the hollow of each peach half and ignite.

Omelette flambée au Cointreau

4 eggs
4 tablespoons Cointreau
4 tablespoons caster sugar
½ oz butter
2 tablespoons jelly marmalade, warmed

Separate the eggs. Mix the yolks with half the liqueur and the sugar. Beat the egg whites until stiff and fold into the yolk mixture until evenly mixed, but quickly and gently to retain as much air as possible. Grease the frying pan lightly with the butter, pour in the mixture and cook as you would an ordinary omelette,

lifting the edges to allow the liquid to run underneath, until just set but still creamy in the centre. Pour the marmalade over it, fold in half, sliding it away from the handle of the pan onto a serving dish. Warm the remaining liqueur in a ladle or small pan, ignite and pour over just before serving.

Sweets and desserts

If a red wine has been served with the main course, persuade your guests to adopt the sensible French custom of eating their cheese first with the rest of the wine and then bring in the dessert, which complements a sweet white wine of considerable roundness and depth. For a simple meal, the milder cheeses, with a fruit platter, prefer a dessert wine – not apples perhaps, but pears, peaches and grapes, or delicately bloomed plums in their season.

Many fresh fruits are delicious marinated and served chilled in wine. Stoned cherries and strawberries in red wine for instance or sliced peaches and pineapple in white wine. If the wine is sparkling, it is best to chill the fruit and the bottle of wine, pouring it over the fruit just before serving to conserve the sparkle.

Orange liqueur ice cream

20 fl oz single cream
4 egg yolks
strip orange rind
4 oz icing sugar
10 fl oz double cream
6 tablespoons Cointreau or Curaçao
finely grated orange zest to decorate

Place the cream, egg yolks and fruit rind in the top of a double boiler and stir constantly until the custard will coat the back of the spoon. Remove from the heat and stir in the sugar until dissolved. Allow to cool. Whip the cream and fold into the cold custard with the liqueur. Place in a shallow container and freeze until firm. Serve scoops of the ice cream in small glass dishes and decorate each with a sprinkling of grated orange zest.

Note: This recipe is equally successful made with cherry brandy, apricot brandy, Kirsch, Grand Marnier or Maraschino instead of Cointreau.

Lemon posset

10 fl oz double cream
2 oz icing sugar, sieved
grated zest and juice of 1 lemon
5 fl oz white wine
1 oz ratafia biscuits, crushed

Whip the cream until thick and gradually whisk in the sugar, lemon juice and zest and the wine. Finally fold in the crushed ratafias and serve in individual glass dishes.

Honeycomb syllabub

10 fl oz double cream
5 fl oz sweet white wine
4 oz caster sugar
2 tablespoons lemon juice
2 egg whites

Whip the cream until thick but not stiff. Gradually beat in the wine, sugar and lemon juice. In another basin beat the egg whites until stiff and fold into the cream mixture. Place the syllabub in individual glass dishes and allow to stand until separated, which will take 12 hours.

Eggnog dessert

3 eggs, separated
2 oz caster sugar
1 tablespoon powdered gelatine
3 tablespoons hot water
10 fl oz hot milk
10 fl oz double cream, whipped
2 tablespoons rum
grated nutmeg to decorate

Place the egg yolks and sugar together in the top of a double boiler and beat together over hot water until thick and pale in colour. Stir the gelatine into the 3 tablespoons of hot water and the milk and when completely dissolved add to the egg yolk mixture and cook, stirring constantly, until smooth. Cool, and when mixture begins to set, fold in the whipped cream, rum and stiffly beaten egg whites. Pile into individual glass dishes and dust with grated nutmeg.

Spiced wine fruit salad

1 lb small strawberries
4 oz seedless grapes
2 peaches, sliced
4 oz redcurrants
4 oz blackcurrants
$\frac{1}{4}-\frac{1}{2}$ teaspoon ground cinnamon
2–4 oz caster sugar
6 tablespoons brandy or 3 tablespoons liqueur

Hull the strawberries and place in a glass dish with the grapes and sliced peaches. Top and tail the currants and add to the dish. Sprinkle with cinnamon and add caster sugar according to your taste and the sweetness of the fruit. Pour over the brandy or liqueur and allow to stand for at least 2 hours. Stir well and serve chilled.

Beignets aux abricots

8 oz flour
1 teaspoon baking powder
2 teaspoons sugar
1 egg
5 fl oz milk
3 tablespoons brandy
1 teaspoon oil
8 oz ripe apricots, halved
oil for frying
icing sugar for dredging

Mix together the flour, baking powder, sugar, egg, milk, brandy and oil and add sufficient water to make a coating batter. Beat well. Remove stones from fruit. Dip apricot halves in batter and fry in deep hot oil until golden brown. Drain and serve hot dredged with icing sugar. The same recipe could be used for ripe plums or pineapple pieces.

Garnet red pears

5 fl oz robust red wine
5 fl oz water
12 oz sugar
1 teaspoon ground cinnamon
pinch salt
8 small dessert pears
4 tablespoons apricot jam
red food colouring

Bring the wine, water, 8 oz sugar, cinnamon and salt to the boil. Peel the pears, leaving the stalks on. Add to the syrup and poach gently for 10 minutes. Remove pears from syrup and chill. Add remaining sugar to syrup in pan and heat until sugar has melted. Boil until reduced by one third, add the jam and tint with red food colouring. Warm sauce through, sieve and pour over the pears to glaze.

Wine and fruit sorbet

12 oz sugar
10 fl oz water
5 fl oz sweet white wine
1 orange
2 lemons
2 egg whites

Dissolve the sugar in the water and boil for 5 minutes. Remove from the heat and add the wine. Grate the zest from the fruit and squeeze the juice. Stir these into the syrup. Leave until nearly cold, then strain into freezing trays. Freeze for about 2 hours, or until mushy but not hard. Beat well, fold in the stiffly beaten egg whites and freeze again.

Note: For long term storage, freeze in individual portions, such as polythene dessert dishes or pretty miniature soufflé dishes. These can be taken straight to the table.

Punsch crème

5 egg yolks
4 oz caster sugar
5 fl oz white wine
2 tablespoons lemon juice
3 tablespoons rum
1 teaspoon finely grated orange zest
12 glacé cherries, chopped
1 oz ratafias

Whisk the egg yolks and sugar together in a double boiler until foamy. Add the wine, lemon juice, rum and orange zest and beat until thick and nearly boiling. Remove from the heat and fold in the chopped cherries and ratafias. Serve immediately in punch glasses.

Claret jelly

20 fl oz red Bordeaux wine
4 tablespoons sugar
1 inch stick cinnamon
2 cloves
good pinch ground ginger
good pinch grated nutmeg
½ oz gelatine
4 tablespoons hot water
5 fl oz double cream, whipped, to decorate
1 oz hazelnuts, chopped, to decorate

Bring the wine slowly to the boil with the sugar and spices, then boil rapidly for about 4 minutes, until slightly reduced. Dissolve the gelatine in the hot water, strain the spiced wine into this and stir well. Cool slightly, pour into small wine glasses and allow to set. Decorate with piped rosettes of whipped cream and sprinkle with the chopped nuts.

Fruit compôte à la Veuve

6 oz caster sugar
2 tablespoons lemon juice
2 tablespoons brandy
1 fresh pineapple, peeled, cored and diced
8 oz sweet white grapes, peeled and seeded
4 ripe peaches, peeled and sliced
5 fl oz sparkling white wine (which need not be Champagne)

Dissolve the sugar by stirring into the lemon juice and brandy. Put this into a pretty glass serving dish. As you prepare the fruit (which should be sufficient to make about 40 fl oz together, in whatever proportions are available) add to the syrup to prevent discoloration. Chill. Just before serving, pour over the sparkling wine. (Serves 6.)

Bananas Martinique

8 medium bananas
1 oz butter
1½ oz brown sugar
finely grated zest of 1 orange
5 fl oz orange juice
½ teaspoon ground cinnamon
7 tablespoons sweet sherry

Peel the bananas, slice in half lengthways and lay in a shallow buttered ovenproof dish. Combine the sugar, orange zest and juice, the cinnamon and sherry. Heat through in a small pan and pour over the bananas. Dot with remaining butter and bake in a moderately hot oven (375°F, 190°C, Gas Mark 5) for 10 minutes. Serve with whipped cream. For special occasions, heat 4 tablespoons rum in a ladle or small pan, ignite, pour over the bananas and serve *flambées*.

A choice trifle

2 tablespoons raspberry jam
2 tablespoons orange marmalade
8 sponge cakes
4 tablespoons sherry
10 fl oz double cream
2 tablespoons brandy
2 oz icing sugar
1 oz split almonds, toasted

Mix together the jam and marmalade and place in the bottom of a glass serving dish. Cover with the sponge cakes and pour over the sherry. Half whip the cream, add the brandy and continue beating, sprinkling in the icing sugar until very thick. Spread over the sponge cakes and allow to set. Spike all over with the toasted almonds.

Sabayon Rose

Note: This is a very old recipe (hence the coy title), considerably predating the trifle of today, which, with its thick layer of custard, is more economical.

French crèpes

batter:
8 oz flour
1 tablespoon icing sugar
pinch salt
3 eggs
15 fl oz milk
1 tablespoon brandy
1 tablespoon oil
butter for frying

filling 1:
4 canned pineapple rings, chopped
2 tablespoons apricot jam
1 tablespoon Cointreau

filling 2:
6 oz can pitted cherries, chopped
2 tablespoons raspberry jelly
1 tablespoon Kirsch

syrup:
4 tablespoons canned fruit syrup
1 oz butter
1 tablespoon caster sugar
2 tablespoons brandy

Sieve the flour, sugar and salt into a bowl and make a well in the centre. Drop in the eggs and half the milk and beat well until smooth. Gradually beat in the remaining milk and finally the brandy and oil. Allow to stand for 15 minutes. To make the filling, mix all ingredients together. Heat a very little butter in a pan and pour in 2 tablespoons crèpe batter, swirling it round the pan to give a thin coating. When bubbles appear on the surface, turn and cook on other side until golden brown. Spread with a little filling, fold in half

then in half again and keep hot. When all the crèpes are cooked and filled, pour the fruit syrup into a chafing dish with 1 oz butter and cook to reduce slightly. Add the sugar and when dissolved put in the folded crèpes and reheat, spooning the syrup over them. Warm the brandy in a ladle or small pan, ignite and pour over the crèpes. Serve as soon as the flames have died down.

Marquise au chocolat

8 oz plain dark chocolate
3 oz butter, softened
2 tablespoons icing sugar
4 egg yolks
3 egg whites
1 tablespoon brandy

Melt the chocolate in the top of a double boiler. Remove from heat and gradually beat in the butter, sugar and the egg yolks, one at a time. Beat the egg whites until stiff, gently fold into the chocolate mixture, adding the brandy towards the end. Pour into a glass serving dish and chill.

Fresh pineapple in rum

1 ripe pineapple
4 oz butter
1½ tablespoons brown sugar
4 tablespoons rum
10 fl oz double cream

Peel the pineapple, remove hard core and dice the flesh. Heat the butter in a frying pan and use to sauté the pineapple until golden brown. Sprinkle with sugar and rum and cook until all the liquid is absorbed. Stir in the cream and serve as soon as the mixture is hot. Drained canned pineapple can be used instead.

Zwetschgen creme

12 oz prunes
5 fl oz sweet white wine
1 tablespoon lemon juice
1 teaspoon finely grated lemon zest
3 eggs
3 oz caster sugar

Place prunes in a saucepan, cover with cold water and allow to soak until plump. Bring to the boil, cover and cook until soft. Drain and reserve cooking liquid. Remove stones and sieve or liquidize the prunes. Mix the resulting purée with the reserved liquid, the wine, and make up to 20 fl oz, adding extra water if necessary. Bring to the boil with the lemon juice and zest. Meanwhile, whisk together the eggs and sugar in a double boiler until foamy. Remove from the heat and fold in the hot prune mixture. Pour into a dish and cool, stirring occasionally. Serve in individual glass dishes.

Fresh figs Olympia

12 fresh figs, just ripe
10 fl oz sweet white wine
7 tablespoons clear honey
15 fl oz double cream
1 oz icing sugar, sieved

Remove stems and arrange figs in a shallow ovenproof dish. Place the wine in a saucepan with the honey, bring to the boil and pour over the figs. Cover dish with foil and put in a moderate oven (350°F, 180°C, Gas Mark 4) for 15 to 20 minutes, or until figs are tender. Chill. Half whip the cream, sprinkle in the icing sugar and whip until really thick but not stiff. Serve the figs in their syrup, crowned with cream.

Canon Bennett's cream

10 fl oz milk
10 fl oz single cream
2 tablespoons caster sugar
1 tablespoon brandy
1 teaspoon rennet
ground cinnamon to decorate

Place the milk and cream in a saucepan and warm to blood heat. Add the sugar and stir until dissolved, then add the brandy. Pour into a glass serving dish, put in rennet and stir. Leave undisturbed until set. Dust the surface with ground cinnamon and serve with whipped double or clotted cream.

Portuguese trifle

2 packets boudoir biscuits
5 fl oz semi-sparkling vinho verde
2 oz glacé cherries
4 oz plain chocolate
1 tablespoon water
10 fl oz double cream

Arrange a layer of boudoir biscuits in the bottom of a glass serving dish and moisten with a little wine. Arrange the rest of the biscuits round the sides of the dish, dipping each one quickly into the wine first. Pour any remaining wine into the bottom. Chop half the cherries and sprinkle in. Melt the chocolate in the top of a double boiler with a tablespoon water. Whip the cream until it forms soft peaks. Fold in some of the melted chocolate, turn into the dish and pour the remaining chocolate in a swirl over the top. Decorate the edge of the dish with the remaining glacé cherries, halved.

Savarin aux fruits

1 teaspoon sugar
generous $\frac{1}{4}$ oz dried yeast
scant 10 fl oz warm milk
6 oz plain flour
3 eggs, beaten
3 oz butter, melted
wine syrup:
8 tablespoons red wine
8 tablespoons caster sugar

To make the yeast liquid, mix together the sugar and yeast until creamy, add the milk, sprinkle surface with flour and allow to stand in a warm place until frothy, about 15 minutes. Sieve the flour into a warm bowl, make a well in the centre and pour in the yeast liquid, eggs and butter. Beat well until smooth and pour into a greased 9 inch ring mould. Cover with greased foil or polythene and allow to rise until it almost reaches the top of the mould. Bake in a hot oven (425°F, 220°C, Gas Mark 7) for 15 minutes. Reduce heat to moderately hot (375°F, 190°C, Gas Mark 5) for a further 10 to 15 minutes. Meanwhile, make the wine syrup. Place the wine and sugar in a saucepan and heat without stirring until the sugar has dissolved. Bring to the boil and reduce by about one third. Take the mould from the oven, turn out the savarin and spoon the hot syrup carefully over until it is all absorbed. Cool, lift on to a serving dish.

The centre of the savarin may be filled with whipped cream, a mixture of fresh fruits, grapes, pineapple and any other fruits suitable to be glazed with sugar syrup. The same wine syrup used for soaking the savarin may be reduced and used for this purpose. The syrup may also be varied by substituting white wine plus a small amount of fruit liqueur, sherry or brandy. This is an excellent method of using up a small quantity remaining in a bottle.

Sabayon rose

5 egg yolks
5 rounded tablespoons caster sugar
4 tablespoons Portuguese rosé wine
1 tablespoon port
rose petals to decorate

Beat together the egg yolks and sugar in a double boiler over gently boiling water, until pale and foamy. Add the wine and port and continue whisking until at least doubled in volume and leaving a strong 'tail' from the whisk. Pile into four glasses and serve warm, each one topped with a rose petal.

Pesche ripieni

4 large yellow peaches
1 oz butter, softened
1 tablespoon icing sugar, sieved
3 tablespoons ground almonds
3 tablespoons crushed ratafias
1 tablespoon chopped glacé cherries
1 egg, separated
5 fl oz sweet white wine
5 fl oz double cream, whipped

Peel the peaches, halve them and remove the stones. Combine the softened butter, icing sugar, ground almonds, crushed ratafias, chopped cherries and the egg yolk until well mixed. Beat the egg white until stiff and fold into the mixture. Arrange the peach halves, filled with the stuffing cut side up, in a shallow ovenproof dish. Pour the wine over and round the fruit (not over the stuffing) and place in a moderate oven (350°F, 180°C, Gas Mark 4) for 15 minutes. Serve with cream.

All sorts of Parties

Parties can be riotous fun for everyone involved except the hostess, who is nearly always too busy to enjoy herself much. But they can be a dead bore for everyone. It takes a lot of imagination and careful planning to ensure that you and your guests have a wonderful time.

My idea of a heavenly party is one where there is a place to sit if I want to, room to stand if I don't, implements adequate to eat the food provided, and drinks I enjoy. These do not include warm white wine. Nor can I cope with risotto to be eaten with a sort of cardboard paddle – even if I had a third hand to wield it, as well as the two I'm using to hold the plate and the glass. As an inveterate party-giver and one who has sometimes suffered at other people's parties, I offer the following advice.

1. Budget for your party and plan the menu accordingly; why envisage smoked salmon on a tinned tuna bank balance.

2. Try to make your menu a little different. It is an effort to greet the sight of a table spread with sausage rolls, sardine sandwiches and trifle with cries of delighted surprise.

3. Be realistic about the number of people you invite and the facilities available. You must have enough of everything; food, drink, glasses, eating implements, and places to put it all down while people *are* eating and drinking. Even a multitude of ashtrays, to protect your carpet from ground-in cigarette ends! If it is a dinner party, do not overcrowd the place settings so that once a glass has been lifted your guest has to search anxiously amongst a riot of floral decorations, candlesticks and salt cellars to find the few square inches from which it came.

4. Where buffet parties are concerned, the great thing is to have the food fresh and this means that it is no use setting out plates of sandwiches, etc., uncovered in a hot room hours before the party begins. The bread hardens, the edges begin to curl and the fillings to fade. It is infinitely better to prepare big foil packs of sandwiches, and sealed polythene food containers of more delicate items, and of garnishes such as parsley sprigs and tomato waterlilies. Keep them in a cool place, have a pile of serving plates ready, and it takes very little time to spread out and garnish the goodies at the last moment.

5. Menu planning for a successful dinner party involves working out a timetable. If there is a sauce with the main dish, can you complete the cooking, and actually make the sauce before your guests arrive? It is hard on the host if he has to keep the conversation going while you dash out, dish up, and actually make the sauce, shouting merry words of encouragement to the guests from the kitchen.

Party ideas from abroad

Holidays outside our own country make it obvious that our parties are pretty pale affairs compared with the merrymaking of our European neighbours, the food and drink provided, and the general atmosphere of *joie de vivre*. Now that the basic cheese and wine party is no longer considered a daring adventure in entertaining, it is time we looked around for other ways to present a party spread without spending a fortune. All these parties are planned on a budget, which I feel is realistic, for though we love our friends, we do not wish to ruin ourselves every time we feel like having a few people round for the evening.

Swiss fondue party

For a small, intimate party, as an alternative to the more formal dinner, this is an ideal way of entertaining friends. You do need a heavy-based pan which you can keep warm over a spirit cooker or chafing dish, and as it is not practical to make enough for more than eight, even if your dish is a big one, this limits the numbers you can serve. There are lots of fascinating customs associated with the Swiss fondue but let us start with the basic recipe. The special pan used in Switzerland is known as a 'caquelon' but any large shallow fireproof dish made of cast iron and enamelled will do.

Neuchâtel fondue

1 clove garlic
½ bottle dry white wine
1–2 teaspoons lemon juice
8 oz Gruyère cheese, grated
8 oz Emmenthal cheese, grated
4 teaspoons cornflour
good pinch freshly ground black pepper
good pinch grated nutmeg
2 tablespoons Kirsch

Rub the inside of the pan with the cut clove of garlic. Pour in the wine, plus a little lemon juice, more if the wine is on the sweet side. Add the grated cheese and place over moderate heat. Begin stirring, and as the cheese melts, sprinkle in the cornflour, pepper and nutmeg. Keep stirring vigorously until the fondue is a thin creamy consistency, add the Kirsch, and transfer from the stove to the spirit burner. This is only intended to keep the fondue warm, without cooking it further, but it will get much thicker from this moment onwards. It needs constant stirring to prevent it from going stringy so invite your guests to spear cubes of bread on their long-handled fondue forks and stir the fondue with the bread in a figure of eight before eating it. This quantity serves four, but if doubled to serve eight will not overfill the fondue dish.

The table should be set with a gay cloth but preferably red, and white china (the Swiss national colours). Provide a place for each person, a wine glass for white wine, a liqueur glass for Kirsch, baskets of fresh crusty bread cut into cubes and individual fondue forks. If you are not drinking wine, it is usual to serve tea with lemon, but certainly never beer. If you have no Kirsch available, vodka makes a very acceptable substitute.

The guests must begin eating at once, as many as possible stirring cubes of bread at the same time and inevitably some people will drop their cubes into the fondue. There are traditional penalties for this. If a lady is the culprit, she has to kiss all the men in the party. If it is a man, he has to buy another bottle of wine. For either sex, the penalty for a second offence is to give another fondue party and invite all present. Halfway through the party, a toast is drunk, known as the *'Coupe de milieu'*. The wine ought to be Neuchâtel, but need not be sparkling. As a concession to dieters, apple cubes may be offered as an alternative to bread.

Since this is the kind of informal supper party which is often arranged on the spur of the moment, children are likely to be present and there is not enough alcohol in the fondue to do them the least harm.

The Swiss Cheese Union, The Swiss Centre, 10 Wardour Street, London, W.1. will send you a free party pack on request, containing a poster, 24 cocktail flags, 4 decorative table mats and their fondue leaflet.

French cheese and wine party

The arrival of the year's Beaujolais 'Nouveau' might well be the excuse for a French cheese and wine party. Otherwise, provide litre or even bigger bottles of French vin ordinaire, remembering that red, rosé and fairly sweet white wines go better with cheese than dry white wines. Reckon 4 or 5 oz cheese per person, and half a small French loaf, or one large loaf for four people. Rolls of fresh Normandy butter look good on the table – each person will take about 1 oz. A litre bottle of wine should serve four people. Dry cider is great with cheese too.

Selection of cheeses
Start with mild flavours from each family of cheese. Among the *cream cheeses*, Demi-Sel is popular, Petit Suisse and the herb or garlic flavoured ones such as Boursin. Then, if the party is a large one, a whole Brie, or at least a really large wedge, and a Camembert. From the same family, Brie, Coulommiers or Carré de l'Est, (milder than Camembert) might appeal. Pont l'Évêque is more mature, and is my personal favourite.

Now for the *semi-hard* cheeses, Livarot is attractive, being pinkish, brown or red in colour, and tied with reeds. Another eye-catcher is Grape cheese, with its overcoat of crunchy grape pips; ask for Tôme aux raisins. Or you might choose the delicately flavoured Port Salut instead. *Blue cheeses* are essential to round out the selection. Bleu de Bresses is not expensive, but the pride of place must go to Roquefort, which is! For the few who really enjoy *goats' milk cheeses*, I suggest Valençay or Saint-Maure.

Selection of wines
If you prefer to buy by the bottle rather than the litre, Sancerre, and a fairly sweet

Entre Deux Mers: A drier white, perhaps an Alsatian Sylvaner, or a rosé – Rosé d'Anjou. Plenty of red – Médoc, Beaune, and a lighter Mâcon Rouge.

Presentation of the table
Arrange the wines and cheeses at opposite ends of one large table, or on two separate tables. It is better if the tables stand away from the wall, so that guests can walk all round to help themselves. Plates, napkins, baskets of bread (and a discreet display of crispbread for dieters) knives, butter dishes – not all together, but spread out so that everyone can help themselves without difficulty. The wine should be served warm or chilled, and opened at the right time, according to the colour, and someone made responsible for offering it. Guests themselves tend to overfill glasses and spill wine while talking.

Serving instructions for cheese
Cream cheese should be served straight from the refrigerator. Others should be taken out at least an hour beforehand to regain their full flavour, Brie and Camembert 2 hours beforehand. Petit Suisse is served with either salt or sugar.

It is a tactful gesture to cut small portions of cheese as 'starters', removing the crusts from these portions if they are not intended to be eaten, as faced with unfamiliar cheeses, people are inclined to munch their way through the lot, crust and all, or avoid them.

The centrepiece of the table ought to be a magnificent platter of fruit which goes well with cheese – apples, pears, peaches, grapes, plums and greengages. Only cream cheeses harmonize with citrus fruits, pineapple or soft berry fruits.

Food from France, 14 Berkeley Street, London, W.1. will send you a free Party Pack on request containing posters, including some showing which French wine goes with which cheese, flags and tricolour ribbon for table decorations.

Austrian glühwein and gulasch party

One does not have to take a skiing holiday to appreciate the delights, in cold weather, of a mug of hot glühwein, or a bowl of gulasch soup. But there must be a restaurant serving both at the top of every ski lift in Austria. Like the Swiss fondue, this kind of fare fits in well with our own winter weather pattern. Mugs are better than glasses for glühwein, which is often served in a jug or pitcher, to keep it hot for drinking out of doors. Gulasch is best eaten out of soup plates, and this recipe with potatoes makes it a main dish. It would be a source of admiration to your guests if you went to the trouble of serving real Austrian dumplings as well. To follow, I suggest another typical Austrian speciality (often described as German but this is not so) Apfel strudel, served cold with whipped cream and lashings of hot, strong black coffee.

Selection of wines
Austria produces mainly white wines. Some average quality red wine is imported from the Baden region of Germany but do not strain too hard after authenticity. I find a generic Bordeaux red suitable for both the drink and the dish. A hard-hitting alternative is Hungarian Bulls Blood.

In Austria, the favourite table decoration would be a carved and painted wooden 'wheel without spokes' with holes all round it filled with candles. If you can't even raise a cow bell to tinkle, invest in a long playing record of yodelling songs, interspersed with the thumping and rump-slapping of local folk dances.

Rich wine gulasch

8 oz fat bacon, diced
6 large onions, chopped
4 lbs braising steak, cubed
salt
4 bay leaves
1 tablespoon paprika pepper
2 tablespoons flour
20 fl oz robust red wine
approximately 20 fl oz stock
3 lbs potatoes, diced

Place the bacon in a large flameproof casserole and fry until golden and the fat runs freely. Add the onion and fry gently until soft but not coloured. Put in the meat and brown on all sides. Add salt, bay leaves, paprika and flour and stir over heat for 2 minutes. Gradually add the wine and enough stock to cover. Bring to the boil, cover and simmer for 1½ to 2 hours, until the meat is tender. Add the diced potatoes 30 minutes before the end of cooking time.

Griebenknödel

4 oz thick streaky bacon
1 lb hot boiled potatoes
2 oz flour
2 eggs
salt
a little milk

Derind the bacon and cut into small dice. Render out the fat in a frying pan until crisp. Drain well. Mash the hot boiled potatoes. Sift the flour and mix with the mashed potato, eggs, salt and milk to make a pliable dough. Knead until bubbles form under the surface. Knead in the bacon dice. Scoop out dumplings with a wet dessertspoon about an inch in dia-meter. Simmer dumplings in boiling salted water for about 20 minutes, until they are light and rise to the surface. Drain well and serve with the Gulasch.

Apfel strudel

paste:
1 lb plain flour
2 teaspoons salt
2 eggs
5 fl oz warm water
2 oz butter, melted

filling:
4 lbs cooking apples
4 oz ground almonds
8 oz sultanas
4 oz fresh white breadcrumbs
8 oz brown sugar
1 tablespoon ground mixed spice
2 lemons
4 oz butter, melted
2 oz icing sugar to decorate

To make the strudel paste, sieve the flour and salt together into a bowl and make a well in the centre. Drop in the eggs, water and the melted butter. Using the fingers of one hand, gradually draw the flour into the liquid using a circular movement. Knead paste lightly until it is smooth and elastic. Leave in bowl, cover with a cloth and allow to stand in a warm place for 15 minutes. Meanwhile, make the filling. Peel, core and slice the apples into a bowl. Add the almonds, sultanas, breadcrumbs, sugar and spices. Grate the zest from the lemons finely and add to the mixture with the juice. Cover the table with a clean cloth and dust lightly with flour. Place the ball of dough in the centre and brush with melted butter. Roll out as thinly as possible, then stretch the dough with your hands, pulling it in all directions towards the edge of the table. It should become paper thin and you should be able to see the pattern of the cloth through it. Allow to rest for a further 10 minutes, then brush with melted butter and spread over the filling. Lift the paste with the cloth and carefully roll it up tightly. Cut the roll in half, shape each half into a horseshoe shape and place on a greased baking sheet with the join underneath. Brush strudels with butter and bake in a moderately hot oven (375°F, 190°C, Gas Mark 5) for about 40 minutes, brushing again with melted butter twice during this time, until crisp and pale golden brown. Dredge with icing sugar and serve slices with whipped cream.

Glühwein

---

grated zest of ½ lemon
2 oz sugar
3 cloves
¼ cinnamon stick
5 fl oz water
1 litre red wine
little orange or lemon juice

Place the lemon zest, sugar, cloves and cinnamon stick in a pan with the water and bring to the boil. Remove from heat and leave to infuse for 30 minutes. Strain, add wine and heat to just below boiling point. Add a little orange or lemon juice to taste.

French Glühwein
Use Bordeaux with cinnamon, nutmeg and bay leaves instead of cloves.

Seehund
Use white instead of red wine and according to the dryness of the wine add more or less lemon juice.

Honey Glühwein
Heat red wine with 5 fl oz honey, cinnamon and 2 slices lemon, (using 1 litre wine and 5 fl oz water).

German wein und wurst party

Those who prefer salami to the pallid paste sandwich will appreciate a wurst party. Nothing fancy is required. Well scrubbed trestle tables are preferable exposed, rather than shrouded in embroidered tablecloths, and the garden is the perfect location. Set your bread boards with soldier-like parades of sliced light and dark rye breads, not forgetting Kummelbrot, the kind with caraway seeds. Butter should be softened slightly, whipped up, then pressed into pots and the tops decorated with the rounded tip of a knife blade to resemble roses. Press in and draw up the tip of the knife to make each petal. The selection of wurst will depend on the resources of your local delicatessen, but at least six are needed to make a nice show, sliced and ready to spread or use as toppings for well-buttered bread.

Reckon on allowing 6 oz sausage, and at least 4 slices of bread per person. Small rye loaves provide the most manageable sizes, and you get about 8 slices from each loaf, so a small loaf serves 2. Large rye loaves will serve 4. Each person will use about 1 oz of butter. To serve 12, buy 2½ lbs of sausage. Aim for variety. Choose from this selection of sausages and pickles.

Selection of sausages
Knackwurst – hard, dry sausage
Leberwurst – smoked liver sausage
Blutwurst – black pudding
Cervelatwurst – pink fairly soft sausage
Salami – the dark Hungarian or Italian
Lachs schinken – smoked loin of pork
Jagdwurst – soft pink spreading sausage

Frankfurter sausages and
Kochwurst (ring) are both to be boiled.

Cucumber pickles
Senfgurken – green, in brine, with mustard seed
Dillgurken – yellow, large cucumber pieces in brine with dill weed and seed
Pfeffergurken – gherkins
Saure Gurken – gherkins in vinegar, with herbs
Spread a few pots of German mustard around amidst the piles of plates, napkins and cutlery.

Selection of wines
Serve each guest on arrival with a Vierteler – $\frac{1}{4}$ litre of white wine. It should be a Rhine wine, a Hochheimer would be perfect, or any other fruity dry white wine. If appetites are Teutonic, the wine consumption is likely to be titanic, so provide sufficient for another Vierteler for each guest if required. So they would want at least five bottles between them.

Kartoffelsalat

1½ lbs potatoes, unpeeled
1 chicken stock cube
5 fl oz dry white wine
5 fl oz mayonnaise
1 tablespoon finely chopped parsley
1 tablespoon finely chopped gherkins

Cook the potatoes in their skins, until just tender. Cool slightly, peel and slice roughly. Have ready the chicken stock cube dissolved in the warmed wine. Pour over the potatoes while they are still hot enough to absorb the liquid. Fold in the mayonnaise, parsley and gherkins. This can be served still slightly warm with hot frankfurters, or cold as part of a mixed hors d'oeuvre, with the sausages sliced and folded into the salad.

Schwarzwaldkirschtorte

---

4 oz caster sugar
3 eggs
4 oz butter, melted
3 oz plain flour
½ teaspoon baking powder
filling:
2 lbs ripe black cherries, stoned
6 oz caster sugar
6 tablespoons Kirsch
10 fl oz double cream, whipped
1 oz plain chocolate, grated

Grease two 7-inch sandwich tins and line the bases. Place the sugar and eggs in a bowl over a pan of hot water and whisk until thick and pale in colour. Remove from the heat and continue whisking until the mixture is cold. Melt the butter and allow it to cool but not to become solid. Sieve the flour and baking powder together and fold into the egg mixture gently. Lastly fold in the melted butter. Divide the mixture between the prepared tins and bake in the top third of a moderate oven (350°F, 180°C, Gas Mark 4) for about 15 minutes, until firm. Cool on a wire rack, then split each cake in half to make four layers in all. To make the filling, place the cherries, sugar and Kirsch in a saucepan and allow to stand for 2 hours. Stir well and gently heat the mixture to boiling point, then cool. Place one layer of sponge on a serving dish and spoon about one third of the cherry filling into the centre. Pipe a circle of whipped cream round the edge and place the next sponge layer on top. Press down lightly and repeat with more cherry mixture and cream until the last sponge layer is put on top. Mask the sides and top of the cake with the remaining cream and sprinkle with grated chocolate.

Italian pasta or risotto party

Italian dishes are particularly suitable for light-hearted entertaining on a small budget. Rich sauces go a long way with mountains of freshly cooked pasta; and risottos, although they may contain some expensive ingredients, are composed mainly of rice.

Allow 4 oz of uncooked pasta per person, so that they may try a little pasta with each of the different sauces. Spaghetti is the traditional choice, but there is an infinite variety of shapes large and small, green and white, the green tinted with spinach juice. The sauces are easily made in advance and reheated in the oven; I suggest cooking three varieties of pasta in separate pans. This would be sufficient to serve 12 people amply, and is an easy quantity to multiply for larger parties.

The three risotto recipes are also designed to serve 12, on the principle that 2 oz of rice is not quite sufficient for one person. The same wines which accompany pasta are recommended with risotto. Litre and two-litre bottles are happily available in red, white and pink Italian wines but it is suggested below that some of the traditional flasks are used because they add a delightful air of gaiety to the setting.

Selection of wines
The Italian flasks in their protective wickered coatings are so attractive that they make a table decoration in themselves. Empty ones make excellent candle holders and a candlelit pasta party is great fun. Red or white candles look best, and have more candles ready so that empty bottles can be pressed into service immediately for illumination. Red Chianti is available in litre size *fiaschi* although the finer Chianti Classico is generally sold in bottles. The labels bear a black cockerel.

If you like white Chianti ask for Tuscan bianco. With pasta the fruity dry white Soave or soft light red Valpolicella make good partners.

Three sauces for pasta parties (*quantities are each to accompany 1 lb spaghetti*

To cook spaghetti, have ready a large pan of rapidly boiling salted water. Place a handful upright in the pan, and coil it down into the water as it softens. Stir gently to separate, and cook until just tender, *al dente*, or slightly firm when bitten. A spoonful of oil in the water helps to keep the spaghetti separate. Drain well, turn into a heated serving dish, sprinkle with a little more oil, and lift and turn with spoon and fork to coat the spaghetti with a delicate, gleaming suggestion of a coating, no more.

Salsa alla Bolognese

---

4 tablespoons oil
2 cloves garlic, finely chopped
3 large onions, chopped
6 oz streaky bacon
3 lb minced beef
1 small head of celery, chopped
5 oz can tomato purée
1 teaspoon sugar
1 tablespoon salt
$\frac{1}{4}$ teaspoon freshly ground black pepper
$\frac{1}{2}$ teaspoon mixed dried herbs
20 fl oz red wine

Heat the oil in a large saucepan and use to fry the garlic and onion gently until limp. Remove rind from bacon and chop. Add to the pan with the beef and stir over low heat until browned, then add the celery. Mix remaining ingredients and add. Stir, bring to boil, cover, simmer for 1 hour. Adjust seasoning.

Salsa alla marinara

1 lb shelled prawns or shrimps, chopped
5 fl oz dry white wine
1 mild onion
2 cloves garlic
4 tablespoons olive oil
1 lb very ripe tomatoes, skinned
1 tablespoon brown sugar
¼ teaspoon dried oregano
¼ teaspoon dried basil
2 tablespoons finely chopped parsley
salt and freshly ground black pepper
2 teaspoons cornflour (optional)

Place the shellfish and wine in a small saucepan and bring to the boil. Simmer for 5 minutes. Finely chop the onion and garlic. Heat the oil in another saucepan and use to sauté the onion and garlic until limp but not coloured. Roughly chop the tomatoes and add to the onion with the sugar, herbs and seasoning. Bring to the boil and simmer uncovered for 10 minutes. Add the wine and shellfish mixture to the sauce and continue cooking for a further 10 minutes. Adjust seasoning if necessary. If preferred, thicken the sauce by adding the cornflour, moistened with 2 tablespoons of cold water. The shellfish can be varied, and some mussels could be substituted for some of the prawns.

Salsa alla Bersagliera

1 mild onion
3 tablespoons olive oil
4 oz Italian salami
3 fl oz dry white wine
15 oz can Italian tomatoes, sieved
salt and freshly ground black pepper
2 teaspoons cornflour (optional)
4 oz Mozzarello or Provolone cheese

Chop the onion finely. Heat the oil and use to sauté the onion until golden. Cut the salami into fine strips and add to the pan. Cook, stirring, for a further 2 minutes. Add the wine and cook, stirring until almost completely evaporated. Add the sieved tomatoes. Season to taste and simmer gently for 20 to 25 minutes. Adjust seasoning, and thicken with the cornflour if preferred. Just before serving, cut the cheese into very thin strips, stir it into the sauce and continue cooking just long enough to heat up but not long enough for the cheese to become stringy.

Note: As well as the sauce, grated Parmesan adds the traditional crowning touch to all these spaghetti dishes. Extra butter and chopped parsley never come amiss either. The freezing instructions for Bolognese sauce also apply to the other sauces, as this is an ideal party for freezer owners.

Faustina's risotto

2½ oz butter
1 small onion, chopped
8 oz long grain rice
2 tablespoons tomato purée
5 fl oz dry white wine
10 fl oz hot chicken stock
7 oz can tuna, drained
few chopped black olives to garnish

Melt 2 oz of the butter and use to sauté the onion until golden. Add the rice and cook until just transparent. Combine the tomato purée, white wine and hot stock. Pour over the rice, bring to the boil, cover and simmer until the rice is tender. Flake the drained tuna, stir through the cooked risotto, adjust seasoning and reheat. Serve topped with the remaining butter and a few chopped black olives.

Shellfish risotto

2 sticks celery
1 large onion
4 tablespoons olive oil
12 oz long grain rice
5 fl oz dry white wine
30 fl oz hot chicken stock
1 oz butter
8 oz button mushrooms, halved
4 oz peeled prawns
4 oz peeled scampi
8 oz crab or lobster meat, diced
1 oz parmesan cheese

Chop the celery and onion finely. Heat the oil and use to fry the onion and celery until softened. Add the rice and stir until it becomes transparent. Pour in the wine and let it boil until well reduced, then add stock and cook uncovered until the rice is just tender, about 12 to 15 minutes, adding a little extra stock or water if necessary. Meanwhile in another pan melt the butter and use to sauté the mushrooms quickly for 2 minutes. Add the shellfish and heat through. Add this mixture with the juices to the rice in the pan, stir well and allow to cook until the liquid is absorbed, stirring occasionally. Serve sprinkled with parmesan cheese.

Pickwickian toasted cheese party

When finances hit rock bottom and you feel a party would cheer you up, it is a heartening surprise to find how little it costs to give this one. You will need two toasting loaves for eight people; they are sliced rather thick and you get about 12 slices to each loaf. The quantity of basic rarebit mixture is reckoned on a party for eight and so is the recipe for mulled cider.

Have ready a small dish of capers, one of finely chopped anchovies and one of crisply fried bacon dice. Toast half the bread, keep some warm in the oven and put as many slices as possible under the grill, spread with the cheese mixture and sprinkled with one or other of the garnishes. When golden and bubbling, cut in half diagonally, remove to serving dishes then spread, garnish and grill the rest of the bread. Meanwhile, toast the remaining bread (if you have a toaster) or toast under the grill, then finish in the same way as the first supply.

The only necessary table decoration is a bowl of nicely polished dessert apples, although a jug, (pewter if possible) of celery sticks and some dishes of pickled onions would be in keeping. The apples will probably disappear during the course of the party, which, if you have all the ingredients ready before you leave home, would make a simple but satisfying conclusion to almost any kind of evening out. If expense is not so much of an object, be a bit more expansive on the garnishes to the rarebit. A slice of ham under the cheese mixture makes a change, or a sprinkling of shelled prawns, or some smoked salmon pieces, which cost less than the delicate perfect slices. In any event, time permitting, onion rings dipped in milk and seasoned flour and fried very crisply make an excellent garnish. Time not permitting, rely on parsley sprigs which add a pretty touch of colour. The recipe for mulled brown ale costs more to make but is given as an alternative because it would promote a truly Dickensian sense of well being. Any sort of lantern, the garden kind with a candle inside, or a paraffin lamp, would add to the atmosphere, as would a shovel full of chestnuts ready to roast over an open fire, if you happen to have one. Most of them get burned, but the smell is lovely.

Mr. Pickwick's rarebit

4 oz butter
1 tablespoon dry mustard
1 lb Cheddar cheese, grated
10 fl oz brown ale
salt and freshly ground black pepper

Put all the ingredients together in a saucepan with a thick base. Heat gently, stirring constantly, until mixture is smooth and creamy. Do not overcook.

Mulled cider

3 flagons dry cider (approx. 35 fl oz each)
4 tablespoons brown sugar
2 sliced oranges
4 cloves
¼ teaspoon grated nutmeg
¼ teaspoon ground cinnamon
1 miniature rum

Heat the cider slowly with the sugar, orange slices and spices until almost boiling. Add the rum and serve at once.

Mulled brown ale

1 oz demerara sugar
1 lemon
20 fl oz brown ale
2 tablespoons gin
2 tablespoons rum
4 tablespoons brandy
10 fl oz water
¼ teaspoon ground mixed spice

Place the sugar in a pan. Grate the zest from the lemon and squeeze the juice. Add these to the sugar with the spirits, spices and water. Bring just below boiling point and strain immediately into mugs.

Recipe Index